Quenching Hell

Quenching Hell

The Mystical Theology of William Law

Alan Gregory

SEABURY BOOKS
New York

Seabury Books
An imprint of Church Publishing Incorporated

Library of Congress Cataloging-in-Publication Data

Gregory, Alan P. R., 1955–
    Quenching hell : the mystical theology of William Law / Alan
Gregory.
        p.   cm.
    Includes bibliographical references and index.
    ISBN 978-1-59627-089-3 (pbk.)
    1. Law, William, 1686–1761.   I. Title.
BV5095.L3G74 2008
230′.2092 – dc22

                                                      2008012872

Church Publishing Incorporated
445 Fifth Avenue
New York, NY 10016

www.churchpublishing.com

5 4 3 2 1

To Suzy, always

Contents

Acknowledgments

Since the writing of this book took a little longer than I expected, my indebtedness to the encouragement and counsel of others has grown proportionately. Debra Farrington of Morehouse Publishing accepted and guided my initial proposal and, since then, Nancy Fitzgerald and, more recently, Cynthia Shattuck have taken the manuscript in hand, suggesting revisions and curbing the volume of my enthusiasm for Mr. Law. I am particularly grateful for the way in which Cynthia Shattuck has made up for my tardiness with her timely energies.

To my colleagues at the Episcopal Seminary of the Southwest I owe much. In particular, conversations with Tony Baker and Nathan Jennings have found their way into some of the best parts of this book. Despite all his new duties Dean Douglas Travis, another beneficiary of William Law's wisdom, has found time to encourage me in the final stages of this project. I am also grateful to the kindness of John Bennet Waters, who, though he may never have read a word of William Law, certainly knows a thing or two about the "devout and holy life."

I first read Law in the course of preparing to teach a class on enthusiastic movements in the eighteenth century. I was struck by the students' eager response to *A Serious Call* and am thankful for their discussion. I was also inspired to apply the occasional "hermeneutic of suspicion" to William Law by the student who noted that it was "guys like him" who put her off the church for twenty years! Janice Jones and James Medley did valiant and vital work on footnotes and typographical errors, and the library staff of the Seminary of the Southwest and of the National Library of

Scotland were extraordinarily trusting with the precious things in their charge — some of which I have yet to return.

Lily, my Great Dane and one of God's most beautiful works, snored gently beside me through most of the writing of this book. My children — Eleanor, who brings hope to people most of us fear, Camilla, who has turned to climbing mountains, and Damian, who prays for us all in glory — have given me much more than I have given them. Finally, this book is dedicated to my wife, Suzy, who demonstrates so much faithfulness and love in the adversities and joys of our lives.

Introduction

I first read William Law's *A Serious Call to a Devout and Holy Life* in the summer of 2000. Before I was halfway through the book, I had realized two things. First, my Christian faith was a shambles and I had largely failed to notice it, and second, the remedy for this was almost embarrassingly straightforward. William Law has been called a spiritual rigorist, and he promoted a Christianity of the stern and strenuous kind. That, in his writings, I found a Christian vigor besides which my own faith seemed barely alive is not surprising. However, I also discovered in Law an attractive and hopeful remedy, and this may suggest that somewhere along the way I had started to read the book upside down. One purpose of the present work, other than to show that Law is much less forbidding than is often thought, is to argue that the exacting character of Law's Christianity and this approachability, the steady confidence into which he invites us, derive from the same root and are, rightly understood, inseparable. Their unity, as we will see, Law finds in Jesus, in the One who demands, all the while promising, "My yoke is easy."

My subtitle, "the mystical theology of William Law," requires some explanation. "Mystical," as I use the term here, has its roots in "mystery" and, specifically, in the mystery that Paul refers to in Ephesians 1:9–10:

> God has made known to us in all wisdom and insight the mystery of his will, according to his purpose which he set forth in Christ as a plan for the fullness of time, to unite all this in him, things in heaven and things on earth.

To be "in the mystery," and thus live a "mystical" life, is to be "in Christ," dwelling by faith in the light of this great work of God, reconciling his creation. By the same token, "mystical theology" is reflection upon our formation in this "Mysterium Magnum." Mystical theology asks how we enter, act, and share in this mystery and what we should and should not say of it. This theology seeks to hear what the Spirit of Christ demands of us and how we discern this Spirit from all other spirits, including our own. The mystical theologian strains to articulate the beauty now revealed, the "excellencies of Christ," the ways of restoration, the suffering that they entail, and the "fullness of time" in preparation for us. If this is the stuff of "mystical theology," then certainly William Law taught such a theology. Also, as he is a guide into the mystery of Christ who speaks of what he knows and does so with an authority that the churches have recognized, Law is due the name "mystic" as well.

Since Law came to place much emphasis on the birth of Christ within us — a feature of his writing that especially appealed to eighteenth-century Quakers — we must ask whether or not he wholly succeeds in maintaining the anchor of his theology in Jesus of Nazareth or, as Law puts it, "that which Christ was while on earth." For now, we may acknowledge the centrality of Jesus to Law's vision: all that we have is "from him," and whatever is estranged from him is in darkness under the shadow of death. If Law has a "mystical theology," then its theme is Jesus and the formation of men and women into Jesus' body and likeness. I want to state this at the outset because, as we will see, not everyone has read Law in this way. Critics have argued that Law in his early treatises makes more of our duties than of Jesus' grace, and in his later works more or less ditches consideration of Jesus in favor of the "Christ within." Part of my purpose is to show that these criticisms miss their mark.

Books about William Law are relatively few. This leaves the editor of the most recent and excellent edition of *A Serious Call to a Devout and Holy Life* and *The Spirit of Love* (1978) with little to suggest beyond the brief essays in the back of Stephen Hobhouse's *Selected Mystical Writings of William Law*, published in 1948, and A. Keith Walker's helpful survey of Law's life and work, written in the 1970s.[1] Among older books, J. H. Overton's *William Law: Nonjuror and Mystic*, published in 1881, remains a most readable, suggestive, and attractive biography and guide. Both Walker and Overton follow a chronological path, taking up Law's writings as they appear in the course of his life. My own emphasis is much more thematic than biographical. I hope that the reader will find that this enables a closer grappling with Law's theology as one opening lively possibilities for contemporary faith and practice. This book is something of a conversation with Law in that not only have I dared to disagree with him on a number of issues that he thought important, but also I have extended some of his ideas, trying to sketch the interesting places to which they lead.

Abbreviations

CP   William Law, *A Practical Treatise upon Christian Perfection, The Works of William Law,* vol. 3 (Eugene, OR: Wipf and Stock, repr., 2001).

DK   *The Way to Divine Knowledge: Being Several Dialogues between Humanus, Academicus, Rusticus, and Theophilus* (Kessinger reprint, n.d.).

SC, SL   *A Serious Call to a Devout and Holy Life; The Spirit of Love* (New York: Paulist Press, 1978).

SL   *The Spirit of Prayer, The Works of William Law,* vol. 7 (Eugene, OR: Wipf and Stock, repr., 2001).

"An Unhurried Life"

John Wesley was among those who made the trip to the south London village of Putney seeking spiritual counsel from William Law. He fretted over a wavering member of the Oxford Holy Club. Law advised, "Let him alone."[1] It is a telling exchange. Wesley runs after goodness, organizing, planning, pushing, negotiating, and traveling. "Letting alone" is not his way. Dr. Johnson, who liked Wesley, complained that he was "never at leisure." William Law was no friend to "leisure" either, but, compared to Wesley, his life is unhurried. Law is a man of the study; Wesley is on his horse, or aboard ship, or preaching in the open, or at meetings, or staying at inns, or scheduled beyond nightfall. Law spent his adult life in Putney, tutoring a reluctant Edward Gibbon, and in his home village of King's Cliffe. We find him passing alms to the poor out of his study window, leading family prayers, visiting the village schools, writing his books, walking from the lending library he created, along the lane that leads beside the fields behind his house. His is a full but regular, measured, and unhurried life. In classical terms, the contrast is between the "contemplative" and the "active" paths. Of course, "contemplation" does not exclude action. Law would not count as Christian a life without deeds of love. Nor does contemplation exclude urgency. Law's urgency appears in almost everything he wrote. Not, though, the striving for a national movement, for new practices of evangelism, or for innovative modes of organization: Law is urgent over the persistent and, at its core, invisible crisis that is our divided will and alienated heart. Hell, as we will see, is an inward and desperate burning.

Putney and King's Cliffe

We know little of Law's early life. Born in 1686, the son of a grocer in King's Cliffe, Northamptonshire, by 1712 he is a fellow of Emmanuel College, Cambridge, with duties as a tutor. Ordained deacon now, his ecclesiastical future was decided abruptly in 1716 when the government demanded oaths of loyalty to the Hanoverian monarchy, repudiating the claims of the deposed Stuarts. Believing this to be immoral, and sympathetic to the Stuarts, Law resigned his fellowship and so abandoned any hopes of a church career. He became chaplain to the family of Edward Gibbon and tutor to his son, who in his turn fathered the famous author of *The Decline and Fall of the Roman Empire.* While at Putney, Law wrote the two works that made him famous: *A Practical Treatise upon Christian Perfection* and *A Serious Call to a Devout and Holy Life.* His tutoring work finished, and the elder Gibbon having died, Law lived briefly in London before returning to his home village of King's Cliffe in 1740. Three years later, he was joined by Hester Gibbon, young Edward's sister, and Mrs. Hutchinson, a moderately wealthy widow commended to Law's care by her husband. Under Law's guidance, they attempted a "devout and holy" household, a life of generosity toward others and austerity for themselves. Out of a household income of some three thousand pounds, only about three hundred pounds were spent on its three members, once "needless, vain, and foolish expenses" were excluded by a notably fine moral filter. Much of the rest was given away to those who rolled up to Law's study window every morning. The trio endowed schools, almshouses, and a library, and they gave regularly to the parish's sick, old, and needy. In addition to money and shirts, the latter always "pre-worn" by Law himself, the household distributed both homemade soup and milk from their four cows. Neighbors complained that King's Cliffe had become the star attraction on every tramp's progress through central England. The parish rector inveighed from the pulpit against the reckless givers, and a petition was presented to the local magistrates. The furor abated, partly in the realization that King's Cliffe without William Law would be worse off than with him, and partly, perhaps, because Law and his companions began to exercise a little more judgment. Though it had such moments of controversy, the disciplined, orderly life at King's Cliffe allowed Law time for extensive reading, for learning German, and for a considerable body of writing, including the books in which he makes extensive use of ideas drawn from the German mystic Jacob Boehme.

The Mysticism of Jacob Boehme

Dr. George Cheyne, philosopher and theologian by ambition but truly famed for his treatment of gout, wrote to William Law, at some time between 1733 and 1737, mentioning the anonymous treatise *Faith and Reason Compared: Shewing That Divine Faith and Natural Reason Proceed from Two Different and Distinct Principles in Man*.[2] This was one of those casual moments in a life that prove momentous. *Faith and Reason* introduced Law to the seventeenth-century German Protestant mystic Jacob Boehme. He found some congenial ideas in *Faith and Reason*, such as the superiority of "divine understanding" over human reason, defended partly with support from Boehme's writings. Taking up Boehme for himself, though, proved a challenge: "when I first began to read him, he put me into a perfect sweat." However, Law persisted, intuiting "glimmerings of a deep ground and sense," until he "perceived that my heart felt well and my understanding kept gradually opening." Finally, he "discovered the wonderful treasure that was hid in this field."[3] From then on, all that Law wrote drew upon Boehme's teachings, from which he derived concepts and terms, a way of thinking about nature and its relationship with spirit, and a compelling version of Christianity's master story of creation, fall, and redemption. Though Law, thankfully, remained a far clearer writer than his teacher, Boehme also inspired a new style of argument and presentation.

Faith and Reason Compared introduced Law to Boehme, but he was already a keen and discriminating reader of Christian mystics. He praised the Germans Johannes Tauler and Heinrich Suso, commending them for their humility as well as their teaching. Humility was not so evident in the Flemish mystic Antoinette Bourignon, who claimed that there were "no Christians but herself." Law's library also included a notably well-thumbed edition of the Flemish Johannes Ruysbroeck, and texts by Meister Eckhart. All these writers would have helped prepare Law to appreciate Boehme. Alongside them, though, why did Boehme stand out sufficiently to justify that initial "perfect sweat" induced in Law by reading him? In *A Serious Call* Law had assaulted the complacencies of a nominal Christianity. Boehme had agreed: "The true divine power in man lets itself be seen externally with good works and virtues."[4] A merely "imputed" righteous would not do; "only an inborn, a childlike [righteousness] counts." Christ himself must "win a form in us." This was entirely in keeping with Law's approach to the doctrine of grace. The Lutheran mystic's position with respect to his contemporaries would also have appealed to Law. Boehme was not a scholar; he was largely self-taught, and he was not a member of any social elite, but rather a shoemaker. The earliest English life of Boehme, written by Durand Hotham, was published in 1654, thirty years after the mystic's death. Hotham stresses the poverty of the "poor contemptible shoemaker" and his lack of education. Boehme's parents, he writes,

> were of the poorest sort, yet of sober and honest demeanor. In the year 1575 they had a son, whom they likewise named

Jacob; his education and breeding was suitable to their wealth.[5]

This is pious exaggeration, as is Law's description of Boehme as "mean and illiterate."[6] Boehme's parents were farmers of relatively comfortable means, certainly not abjectly poor, and though Boehme's formal education was limited, he was remarkably well read. He was certainly not simple, if "simple" means unsophisticated, uninformed, or unintelligent. To Law, though, Boehme was a paradigm of God's indifference to the pecking order of worldly pride. Jacob was a man taught of God. Jesus had praised his Father, "Thou hast hid these things from the wise and prudent, and hast revealed them unto babes" (Matt. 11:25). Boehme had showed that this was still God's way.

In 1738, while temporarily settled in London, Law composed *The Grounds and Reasons of Christian Regeneration*, quite a short book of which he remained especially fond. The dominant themes are those of the fall, the ruin that humankind suffered, and the process of redemption that God initiated as soon as Adam fell. The title page announces that the work is offered to "the consideration of Christians and Deists." Deism taught a severely rationalized version of Christianity in which Jesus is reduced to the teacher of moral and religious truths that, were it not for "crafty priests," we might well have discovered without his help. All we needed to do was pay attention to "Nature," contemplate its workings, and conclude to a well-intentioned, morally upright Creator whose physical and ethical laws relieved him of all but watching benignly and granting immortality to the reasonable and good.

Deism remained a preoccupation for Law throughout his life. He saw it as the counterpart and counterfeit of true religion, worldly faith par excellence. Where true Christianity sees God in the world, the Deist affirms God's absence; while true Christianity recognizes creation as expressive of God, Deism sees only a mechanism from which an engineering God may be deduced; and whereas true Christianity settles in the heart, Deism is a religion of mere intellect. Historically, Deism may have been a minority movement, but, in Law's eyes, it disclosed the affliction of modern Christianity: a progressive hardening of the spiritual arteries that obscured the mystery of God and blocked experience of the intimate commerce between divine Spirit and creation.

The year 1740 was a particularly productive one. In addition to moving back to King's Cliffe, Law published three books, including the widely read *An Appeal to All That Doubt, or Disbelieve the Truths of the Gospel, Whether They Be Deists, Arians, Socinians, or Nominal Christians. In Which the True Grounds and Reasons of the Whole Christian Faith and Life Are Plainly and Fully Demonstrated.* The *Appeal* is a brief outline of Christian teaching in which appears its all-encompassing scope, from the being and love of God, through the multiplicity of heavenly and earthly creation, to human tragedy and human redemption in Christ. As the title suggests, Law has specific readers in mind, and he wants to shape his outline of "true Christianity" as a living, convincing alternative both to his old enemy "Deism" and to other contemporary radicalisms: "Socinianism," which denies the Trinity, and "Arianism," which counts Christ as significant for salvation but not as divine.[7] Two features of Law's account loom large, therefore. Against the Socinians and the Arians, Law describes the human tragedy as one that nothing short of God himself, God in our flesh, might redeem. Against the Deists, he takes their central term, "Nature," and reclaims it for Trinitarian Christianity. Yes indeed, he agrees, we must understand everything "according to Nature," and certainly God does not violate "Nature" in any of his works. "Nature," though, is not the Deist's clockwork, a lifeless mechanism, but rather the eternal manifestation and play of God's creative life, the inexhaustible potentialities for life that burst out of the loving movement of Father, Son, and Spirit.

After the *Appeal* Law published nothing for another nine years. Instead, his study hours were taken up with Boehme and with learning the "High Dutch language" necessary to read the original texts.[8] While this intense immersion in Boehme no doubt clarified and strengthened Law's own interpretation, it is striking how little his appropriation of Boehme changed overall. With the exception of the seven "properties" of nature, a theme that he does not begin to introduce until *The Way to Divine Knowledge* and *The Spirit of Love*, both published in 1752, Law's teaching remains remarkably constant.

Between 1749 and 1754, Law completed the fullest statement of his later thought, in the three books: *The Spirit of Prayer* (1749–1750), *The Way to Divine Knowledge* (1752), and *The Spirit of Love* (1752–1754). These pieces also develop his most daring ideas. Law does not trumpet his boldest suggestions, and the meditative style makes it easy to miss how controversial some of his thinking had become: his challenge to a traditional understanding of God's "wrath," for instance, or his insistence on nature as the medium of God's manifestation, or his openness to a hope for universal redemption.

All three works are largely, if not entirely, made up of dialogues. Law's handling of the dialogue form is rather stiff and forced, especially compared with the vivacity of the character sketches included in *A Serious Call*. He conveys little or no sense of conversational drama, and the nonlinear way he chooses to approach his own teaching denies his dialogues significant movement toward a climax. The characters likewise are very much stock figures. There is Academicus, the intellectual whose bookish predilections make him the fall guy for the spiritually more acute; Rusticus, the plain man of the soil; Humanus, the converted Deist; and Eusebius, the pious curate. For the most part, their role is to provide occasion for lengthy expositions from Law's spokesman, Theophilus. Little exchange occurs, except occasionally between Rusticus and the unhappy Academicus. Rusticus, though, is merely an alternative voice for Theophilus, and were it not for Law's keen involvement in village life, this representative of the common man might convince us that Law had never actually met one.[9]

None of this should detract, however, from some superb writing. Law's later prose is often vivid and poetically rich. His language is passionate yet measured so as to achieve dignity, even stateliness, the control intimating reserves of power and depths unspoken. He also retains his ability to focus a point with sudden clarity, so that the generally expansive and loosely structured writing is gathered at moments like the rich material on a comfortable sofa held down and tightened by studs. Even the dialogue, though awkwardly handled, has some advantages. It breaks up the text, allowing Law to pose the questions that open up his teaching and to return to themes from different perspectives, cumulatively enriching them. These themes are elements of what Law understands as the essential structure of Christian truth or, as he would say, the "ground" of faith. This "ground" is first and foremost a story that begins and ends in eternity and makes its way from Eden through Israel to Jesus, who is raised upon the cross, drawing all humanity to himself and his Father. From this story, from its essential themes, arises all that Christians must say and do and be.

By 1756, Law had expounded his theological vision in seven works, the last three of which constituted the major and mature statement of his ideas. His fame as the author of *A Serious Call* made criticism inevitable, especially since the difference of style and content was so immediately striking. The most thorough and extensive critique came from John Wesley, who in January 1756 published his *Open Letter to William Law*. Wesley examined Law's teaching in detail, with numerous quotations from *The Spirit of Prayer* and *The Spirit of Love* in particular. Sadly, Wesley's assessment was so hostile, so driven by what he fears are the effects of Law's teaching, and so dismissive of the "high-flown bombast" and "unintelligible jargon of the mysticks," that though the criticism is extensive, it is not truly serious. Wesley never stops to enquire about what exactly Law is trying to say. His judgment, therefore, remains entirely on the surface. No special talent is needed to find sentences that sound extravagant or strange and pull them from their context as evidence of unintelligibility or confusion. Wesley, though, does little more than that; he lacks interpretative curiosity, having decided in advance that anyone who sounds like Law is sounding has become spiritually unglued. "All life is a desire," he quotes Law, and then he comments, "Might you not just as well have affirmed, all life is a hatchet?"[10] In other words, if it sounds like nonsense to Wesley, it must be nonsense. Wisely, Law made no public reply.

Singing and Dying

In 1757, Law contributed one last book to contemporary theological controversy, this tackling William Warburton's massive work *The Divine Legation of Moses.*[11] Warburton's thesis, argued in agonizingly fulsome detail, is that Israelite religion was unique in having no doctrine of eternal life. Since, Warburton argued, such a doctrine is essential to social order, this demonstrates that Israel was the subject of an "extraordinary providence."[12] Law's vigorous reply accuses Warburton of undermining the unity of Old and New Testaments and so exploding the continuity of God's redemptive work. Humanity under Moses is the same humanity that received Christ, a humanity that longed and hoped for an enduring peace with God. To be sure, the knowledge of what that meant was only foreshadowed in the Old Testament, known in anticipations and shadowy images, but it was known nonetheless, and to suppose otherwise is to divide the whole "process of Christ" that begins with Adam and Eve. This critique of Warburton was the last of several polemical works, the earliest being his first publication, engaging what Law considered fundamental threats to Christian teaching and, therefore, practice. Here, we need to attend in any detail only to one of these books, the anti-Deist *The Case of Reason; or, Natural Religion, Fairly and Fully Stated*, published in 1731, a text that sheds a special light on *A Serious Call*.

Law was seventy-one when his "confutation" of Warburton went to press. He was still intellectually alert, though his last two pieces, the *Of Justification by Faith and Works: A Dialogue between a Methodist and a Churchman* and *An Humble, Earnest, and Affectionate Address to the Clergy* do show signs of weariness and some loss of his nimble way with distinctions and metaphors. The latter, though, does contain a moving and frank statement of Law's opposition to "the murdering Monster of WAR."[13] All human beings, Law argues, have the highest possible vocation: to live in God, enflamed with the Spirit of love. The simple fact of that vocation, set against war's desolating horror, should render us repentant. What "nameless Numbers...are not suffered to stay in this World, till Age and Experience have done their best for them, have helped them to know the inward Voice and Operation of God's Spirit."[14] Whenever Christ is truly king, his church neither "wants, nor allows War."[15]

During these last years, Law and his two companions continued their charitable work in King's Cliffe, establishing almshouses, a home for the schoolmaster, and a public library made up of books from Law's own collection. The collection is now housed in the Northamptonshire record office, but the stone inscription remains above the building in King's Cliffe: "Books of Piety are here Lent to Persons of this and Neighbouring Towns." Conscientious to the end, Law succumbed to a cold while conducting the Easter audit of the two King's Cliffe schools. The sickness developed into a painful infection of the kidneys, and Law died, in much pain, on April 9, 1761. When he was close to death, he sang a hymn with a "strong and very clear voice."[16] That hymn announces the central theme of Law's "mystical theology":

> This day sets forth thy praises, Lord;
> Our grateful hearts to thee shall sing,
> Our thankful lips shall now record,
> Thine ancient love, Eternal King.

Chapter 2 _____

All Law and No Gospel?

William Law's popularity in the eighteenth century rested largely on the two books written relatively early in his literary career. *A Practical Treatise upon Christian Perfection* was published in 1726, and his most famous and consistently reprinted book, *A Serious Call to a Devout and Holy Life*, appeared three years later. On board for Georgia in 1735, nervous of the churning waves and the ship's alarming bangs and creaks, John Wesley read Law's *Christian Perfection* to his queasy fellow passengers.[1] At this stage, the book was foundational for him. He reads it virtually daily, prescribes regular doses of the work for others, and chooses it as a sure guide to "the nature of Christianity." Wesley viewed *A Serious Call* with much the same enthusiasm, writing to Law in 1738 that "for two years (more especially) I have been preaching after the model of your two practical treatises."[2]

Wesley always recommended the "two practical treatises" for the edification of his preachers and for Methodists generally. In the latter part of his career, during a sermon reflecting on the early years of the movement, Wesley was happy to confess, "All the Methodists carefully read these books, and were greatly profited thereby."[3] Nevertheless, on May 14, 1738, he also told Law that the treatises were deeply flawed, flawed as to the substance and foundation of the gospel itself. In a letter, he rebuked Law for omitting to mention that salvation was indeed free. There were "great, wonderful, and holy" things in Law's books, but not the one thing needful.

Wesley was not alone in finding both *Christian Perfection* and *A Serious Call* defective with respect to the ground of salvation. Unlike the author whose anonymous tract of 1728 accused Law of simply casting "a noxious and baleful shade o'er all the comforts of life," evangelical and Methodist critics bridled at implications that salvation was conditional upon our moral efforts.[4] We find the same double judgment that Wesley made. In Law's writings, on the one hand, much is wise and godly; on the other hand, the gospel appears to be standing on its head. George Whitefield, the evangelist who introduced Wesley to field preaching, recognized Law as an incomparable guide to the practical business of Christian life but also considered writing a "gospelized" version of *A Serious Call*.[5] A project along those lines was later realized by Wesley, who published an abridged version of *A Serious Call*. He carves out the passages that suggest a righteousness won by good works. In one of Law's character sketches, "Penitens" (Penitent) describes God's judgment as "where nothing will be rewarded but good works" (*SC* 72). Wesley both omits the offending theology and renames the speaker "Cives" (Citizen), thus dumping him clearly among the worldly. Another evangelical, Thomas Scott, read *A Serious Call* in 1776. Like Dr. Johnson, he began it "carelessly," having previously regarded it "with contempt." The work surprised him, just as it had Johnson: "I had no sooner opened it, than I was struck with the originality of the work, and the spirit and force of argument with which it is written." Law showed him his need of Christ and the shape of Christian commitment, "the practice of that holy diligence in the use of means which the important interests of eternity reasonably demand." He concludes, though, that *A Serious Call* "certainly contains as little gospel as any religious work I am acquainted with."[6] For anyone troubled in soul, fearful over their sins, and needing the comfort of God's mercy, Scott thinks that the book will do harm, as if a celestial health warning should be stamped on every cover.

The critique is serious and turns about the nature of Christian life, its birth, character, and foundation. In theological terms, Law was accused of falling down on the doctrine of "justification." Confidence in our fellowship with God, that we stand as beloved children, not condemned sinners, is based on God's initiative in restoring us while we were "still far off." "Justification" presupposes that our relationship with God is a moral relationship, for the rupturing of which human beings are responsible and, therefore, guilty. However, we do not put ourselves right with God, but rather God puts us right with him, justifies us, making the unrighteous "righteous." By Law's time, the question as to precisely how we are "put right" had generated various explanations in Protestant theology. In simplest terms, justification was absolution or forgiveness of sins. A dominant line of thought, among both Lutherans and Calvinists, insisted that, as we have no righteousness of our own, "all the righteousness of Christ" becomes our justification as it is "freely and fully *imputed* to us." Another emphasis, especially in Calvinist theology, taught that justification occurs through our being "in Christ," "incorporated" or "grafted" into him. Some seventeenth-century Anglicans brought our own holiness under the concept of justification: we are justified, first, by God's forgiveness on the basis of Christ's righteousness and, second, by the righteousness that God's grace works in us. In the eighteenth century, especially in Methodist circles, and among Quakers or those influenced by the Christian mystical tradition, justification was commonly understood as synonymous with "regeneration" or "new birth."[7] Whichever of these interpretations, or combinations of them, were accepted, the red thread of the doctrine was an emphasis on the absolute priority of God's grace. The basis of that fruitful peace between God and ourselves is God's love, extended "while we were yet sinners." Salvation was wholly God's work, both *on* us, "putting us right," establishing our fellowship with God (generally termed "justification"), and *in* us, the Spirit bearing fruit in our lives (generally, "sanctification").

Put bluntly, the doctrine of justification poses us an alternative: does Christ free me to live a holy life, or do I live a holy life so that Christ will free me? The gospel is liberating only if we choose the first option. Freed from the toil of cobbling together our own security in the face of God and a difficult world, we may, because "God first loved us," venture our ambiguous selves in love and neighborliness. For Wesley, Law's "two practical treatises" appeared to take the second alternative. But if God's mercy depends upon my sincerity in trying to be seriously holy, how can I find any "joy and peace in believing"? Certainly, Law made statements that his critics found radioactively dangerous:

> It seems plain, that our salvation depends upon the sincerity and perfection of our endeavours to obtain it. (*SC* 66)

On the other hand, in an early conversation with Wesley, Law had told him, "Religion is the most plain, simple thing in the world; it is only, 'We love Him because He first loved us.' "[8] One possibility, of course, is that *Christian Perfection* and *A Serious Call* invited criticism as godly but dangerous books because their author was unclear and self-contradictory, not having settled his mind on some basic issues. Before we jump to this conclusion, however, especially about a writer so admired for clarity of thought and force of argument, we must look carefully at the works themselves.

Life in the End

Law chose two texts for the title page of *A Serious Call*. The first is a command, "He that hath ears to hear, let him hear" (Luke 8:8). This is addressed to whoever picks up the book. "I know," Law had written in *Christian Perfection*, "of only one common Christianity, which is to be the common means of salvation to all men" (*CP* 1). The demand to hear is issued not to an elect or an elite, but to all. There is no "Christianity Lite," a way by which the majority of us compromised, halfhearted, easily discouraged, and occasionally indifferent Christians can just slip by. Christian "perfection" is such, Law will insist, that "men in *Cloisters* and religious retirements cannot add more, and at the same time such [that] Christians in all states of the world must not be content with less" (*CP* 6). The world goes about its bustle, whirls in inexhaustible distractions, and then there is this voice, the words of Jesus taken up by William Law: "Stop, all of you, whatever you are doing — and hear!"

The time to hear is, of course, now, not when we have time to spare for it, which, of course, we never will. Law's second choice of text shows why the command is peculiarly urgent: "And behold, I come quickly, and my reward is with me" (Rev. 22:12). John's Revelation, of course, opens onto the fulfillment of all God's ways and works, onto the new Jerusalem, the return and reign of Christ the Lamb. What Law has in view, however, is less that final cosmic arrival than the end time that is the death of each one of us. Looked at from one side, my death is my life's end, when as far as my actions are concerned, there is nothing more to be made of it. From the other side, however, my death is the coming of Christ, who has called me, drawn me, guided me, and will yet make much of me.

Our mortality certainly is deniable. We do not deny it as a fact, but we do put much effort into denying it in practice. In regard to death, Law observes,

> the health of our bodies, the passions of our minds, the noise, and hurry, and pleasures, and business of the world, lead us on with eyes that see not, and ears that hear not. (*SC* 69)

Our mortal lives, our very strivings and passionate hopes, invite the questions "Why?" "What is it all for?" Even if some determinedly hardheaded philosopher tells us that such questions are vulgar invitations to talk nonsense, they remain insistent, implied if not pursued. A woman who had survived cancer against the odds given by her physician told me that she had decided that life was too good to waste on anything that she did not want to do. An old friend telephoned my wife: "I'm calling to say good-bye. I have a brain tumor, and I don't know how long my mind will last." She went on, "I also want to warn you not to put things off. I've done that all my life, and now I've run out of time."

"What's the point of it all?" Is this a question that we can answer? There is a long-running human industry for producing answers. A trip to the local bookstore provides us with dozens of titles offering the meaning of life, in one form or another. Innumerable ideologies have had a go at telling us precisely why we are here and what "it" is all in aid of. Christians have good reason to be wary and cautious about these ceaseless projections of meaning, assertive maps of our own significance or insignificance for the universe. It does not take a misanthrope to acknowledge how readily answers to our and the world's mystery serve the convenience of those that propound them, often to the misery of others. Then, again, our passions will give some sort of answer, if our minds do not. Consider one of Law's character sketches:

> Flatus [Wind] is rich and in health, yet always uneasy, and always searching after happiness. Every time you visit him, you find some new project in his head; he is eager upon it as something that is more worth his while, and will do more for him than anything that is already past. Every new thing so seizes him, that if you were to take him from it, he would think himself quite undone. His sanguine temper, and strong passions, promise him so much happiness in everything, that he is always cheated, and is satisfied with nothing. (*SC* 164)

Our minds are fertile in imagined satisfactions, and, as Law warned Wesley, "the heart . . . as being the seat of self-love, is more deceitful than the head."[9] At one very important level, Christians must proclaim a decided "No!" to the whole question of meaning. We cannot judge the worth of our own lives, what time has made of us and we of time. That answer is given us, by the One who is coming, in death, to all of us: "Behold, I come quickly, and my reward is with me."

Of course, that being said, the answer is not simply hidden from us now. It comes in the form of promise and call. Law begins his treatise on Christian perfection by telling us who we truly are, the "point" of human life. We will not understand Law's calling to perfection, and, more importantly, we will perceive it as an appalling burden, a duty "too high" for us, if we fail to see it arising naturally from who we are "in Christ." The definition of "perfection" is businesslike and clearly democratic, a perfection for the whole household of God:

> What can Christian perfection be, but such a right perform-
> ance of all the duties of life, as is according to the laws of
> Christ? What can it be but living in such holy tempers, and
> acting with such dispositions as Christianity requires? (*CP* 6)

We are, then, to conduct ourselves "according to the laws of Christ" in "every state of life." Law is fond of images of sleeping, dreaming, and awakening. Hearing the gospel is like waking up and finding "every man sleeping out of his proper state, some happy, others tormented, and all changing their condition as fast as one foolish dream could succeed another" (*CP* 19). The gospel awakens us to the point of it all, the secret of our making and destiny. From our beginning, and through our restoration in Christ, we are fitted for a "heavenly condition," "participation of the Divine Nature." Christian perfection, then, "living according to the laws of Christ," is not a means to an end; it is, rather, the temporal form of eternal life. If Law's language sometimes suggests that Christian perfection is a means to an end — *how* we attain "eternity" — that is because its practice is the way as well as the goal. We live in our end, which is, on the one hand, death to all that would disappoint us, "the World and worldly tempers," and, on the other hand, Christ, who at our death will complete the end that he has made of us, making us "inhabitants of heavenly and immortal bodies" (*CP* 13).

The practice of Christian perfection is formation in Christ, realized by "the enlivening of the Divine Spirit." As we live toward that perfection, desire it, sigh and groan for it, rejoice as it provokes us, and nurture even its smallest triumphs, our end draws nearer. To put it in the technical language of theology, Law understands Christian perfection *eschatologically.*

William Law's prose, at least in his earlier writings, is almost severely clear. The clarity of his writing, though, is not driven solely by the desire for lucid and reasoned communication — it is theologically motivated. His rhetoric reflects his understanding of sin. Human beings are lost in a wasteland of little things, absorbed in "bubbles," and intent upon vapors. Law writes, therefore, for willfully distracted minds and even shiftier hearts. Thus the style is strikingly direct, and his logic apparently inescapable. Often his illustrations are comically exaggerated, even grotesque. Pride invents "a thousand wants," pursuing them, often ruinously, as if essential to life. The proud person is like "a man racking his brains and studying night and day how to fly . . . bruising himself with continual falls and at last breaking his neck" (*SC* 151).

It All Boils Down to This

Christianity, Law asserts, boils down to "two great truths, the deplorable corruption of human nature, and its new birth in Christ Jesus" (*CP* 13). Is that really all? Surely there is more to Christianity than that. There is indeed, but Law's compression is strategic. Anything more — the doctrines of God, the life and teaching of Jesus, the church and its sacraments, and so on — is none of our business except insofar as we have grasped for ourselves these two truths. What concerns us is our need and the love held out to us. This is the basis for a right concern with the many and varied elements of what we call "the Christian religion." The bald summary, seemingly obviously objectionable, drives the reader back to where Law wants her, which is considering her own responsibility, the condition of her own soul. Theological discussion, Law understood, is as good a distraction from the point, from ourselves, as anything apparently less noble and elevated.

Law has a strong doctrine of sin, the "deplorable corruption of human nature." Human beings are well and truly fallen. Our world is "a mere wilderness, a state of darkness, a vale of misery, where vice and madness, dreams and shadows, variously please, agitate, and torment the short, miserable lives of men" (*CP* 69). Today, many Christians find such dark judgments unpalatable, if not morbid and savagely life-denying. Confronted with a similar passage from *A Serious Call*, one student of mine announced that this was the kind of thing that for many years repelled her from the church. It is a healthy principle, though, to understand such reactions as a call to look more carefully rather than rush to judgment. From the outset, we must hold Law's "two great truths" together: the "deplorable corruption" and the "new birth in Christ Jesus." The darkness of our situation appears in the light of our creation, calling, and redemption. How great is the plight, Law asks, "that should need so great a Mediator," yielding himself in such humility to such a death. We begin to glimpse the depths of our woe, of the corruption that mars God's image, only when we find that we are "temples of the Holy Ghost," summoned to "a participation of the Divine Nature." We can pray for "sinners," including ourselves, only when we know who we are and what God holds out for us. When we let these two truths drift apart, allowing our "deplorable condition" to stand alone, we end up with growling misanthropy or a mean-spirited self-righteousness. Certainly, William Law was not easygoing: he was undoubtedly strict, often somewhat severe, and always demanding. However, I find Law's rigorism more bracing than crushing, more inspiring than disheartening. This is, I think, because he keeps his "two great truths" in close proximity. Our plight is deadly, eternally serious, but it is understood and interpreted through the glory that is offered us.

Law does not develop a distinctive theology of sin in either *Christian Perfection* or *A Serious Call*. He relies on a common understanding shared by his readers and made familiar through worship, preaching, and the many popular texts and manuals of devotion. Law certainly writes about sin as enmity to God, as a disobedience, an "abomination" that provokes God's anger and judgment. Even at this stage, though, Law prefers metaphors that describe a disordered condition: sin is a "disease," "impurity," "defilement," "corruption," a "blemish" on what God has created good. Later in life, he will dramatically reinterpret the theme of God's anger, eliminating any suggestion that it qualifies the constancy and completeness of God's love. Little is said about the fall as such. Law takes for granted a traditional account of Adam's ruin and its consequences, derived largely from St. Augustine. Sin is thus the "weak, miserable, sinful state of all that are descended from fallen Adam." The root of the human calamity, Law insists, is the will. In willing wrongly, in misguided love, lie our ruin and our misery.

Since our will is the source of our problem, Law treats Christian perfection democratically. Perfection, he announces, "calls no one to a *Cloister*" (CP 5). Perfection consists in "necessary Duties, in the Exercise of such holy Tempers *as are equally necessary and equally practicable in all States of Life*" (CP 5 [my emphasis]). There is one standard, applied to all. Christian perfection admits of no criterion of holiness reserved to a few and of which the majority is relieved. The "highest Degree of Christian Perfection . . . is also the lowest Degree of Holiness which the Gospel alloweth" (CP 6). A ready objection is that this runs counter to experience. We no more expect every life to be equally productive of goodness than we expect all persons to show equal wisdom. Circumstances, character, and natural abilities make for wide variations. Law knows this perfectly well, but he is not applying the standard of perfection to the "external Instances and Acts of Virtue, which depend upon outward Causes and Circumstances of Life" (*CP* 41). A person of means and influence may well do more good outwardly than many others in less-favored circumstances. Then, again, she may be generous from utterly self-serving motives. Someone of limited education or understanding may act well but with less insight or tact. On the other hand, she may have greater integrity in her faithfulness to that "Measure of Light and Knowledge which God has given" her. The substance of virtue, of true goodness, is in the cast of the will. Christian perfection consists in "the inward Piety of the Heart and Mind" or, to put it slightly differently, "who or what, and how do you love?" If we're honest, we must admit that even at our best, our motives are an impure mix: integrity of will seems as remarkable as intelligence in sheep. This, though, is why a "devout and holy life" is a school for formation in honest loving. Through a practice of daily dedications, in the mixture of our desires, the Spirit sets the grain of our willing toward God and toward showing his generosity in flesh and blood.

Law handles the traditional teaching on sin so as to focus it upon the audiences that he has in mind. *Christian Perfection* and *A Serious Call* assume a culture in which Christianity is the religious background of people's lives. This society has churches and clergy, laws and governing institutions claiming Christian sanction, and a shared "Christian" morality. Law's intended readers have come to terms with Christianity, found a way of living with it, a compromise between their own hopes and happiness and Christianity's demands. "Julius" is a faithful churchgoer who never misses a Sunday, and yet, Law tells us, his life in all other respects is no different from those who never attend. Law is exhorting not notorious lives but rather the respectable who, when it comes to God, act as if the Lord of life and death is content with the nod of partial allegiance. In *Christian Perfection*, Law began to experiment with character sketches as a means of exemplifying his teaching. He perfects the device in *A Serious Call*, in which the didactic and exhortatory passages are interspersed with sharply drawn and memorable characters. Thus Law finds his description of sin and grace in the faces of eighteenth-century culture. By the time Law was writing, Britain had enjoyed several decades of steadily rising agricultural production and a dramatic increase in overseas trade. New farming methods, including improved fertilization, a more systematic and efficient use of land, and better animal feed, increased confidence, and wealth among landowners had reduced the fear of serious dearth. Higher incomes and stable prices stimulated an unprecedented consumer demand not only from the landowning elite — the aristocracy and gentry — but also from the "middling orders" of lawyers, clergy, and government officials, money men and merchants, skilled artisans, tradesmen, and shopkeepers, such as Law's father. Commercial energies generated and satisfied new desires, new definitions of good taste, respectability, and status, and luxuries became needs.

Law sees this expanding system of supply and demand as taking the shape of our old Adam, recapitulating our ancient perversity. Prosperity funds a rapid inflation of needs. Desires breed more desires, and desires spawn needs that far outstrip any sober judgment of what we really require. We "create a new world of evils and fill human life with imaginary wants and vain disquiets" (*SC* 150).[10] Certainly, Law's notion of our legitimate needs is a narrow one, but he is asking the right question. Since he views human lives eschatologically, in the light of their end, Law exposes sin's irrationality, the shocking perversity of our wills. So, Celia is comfortably provided for, has plenty of company, and is in good health. She enjoys none of it because she is consumed by an irritability alive to the smallest slights and most trivial checks to her will. Flavia's genius is thrift, but her parsimony only serves her fashionable affectations; so conscious is she of appearance that "the rising of a pimple in her face, the sting of a

gnat, will make her keep her room two or three days" (SC 107).[11]
The world of business defines Calidus to such a degree that he
fears retirement and refuses rest.[12] Ingenuity, resourcefulness, and
hard work have made Mundanus (Worldly) rich, but ambition
has stunted his spiritual life, so still "the old man prays now in
that little form of words which his mother used to hear him re-
peat night and morning" (SC 204). As Flatus (Wind) rushes from
one enthusiasm to another, never satisfied, always disappointed,
Succus rolls between bed and the dinner table, and Penitens (Penitent), surprised by death, wonders where his life has gone. In one
of Law's most gruesome touches, Matilda enslaves her daughters
to the demands of fashionable beauty. After her daughter dies
from the disciplines of beautification, her body is examined, and
"it appeared that her ribs had grown into her liver, and that her
other entrails were much hurt by being crushed together with her
stays, which her mother had ordered to be twitched so strait"
(SC 265).

These characters, sad, absurd, trivial, sinister, or grotesque, are
bound to a wheel of satisfactions that do not satisfy. Law's characters are not complete strangers to piety: Julius and Eusebius are
devout in church, Flavia respects the Sabbath, and even Calidus
prays when his ships are at sea. This, though, is not Christian
freedom. Rather, these folk are seeking to draw God into the
web of false satisfactions — an easy rest for the conscience, a
cheap sense of righteousness, and an insurance against present
and future disaster.

As sin is a corruption of the will, it goes to the root from which
our lives proceed. The solution, then, must be as radical as the
problem. So Law sets against our "deplorable corruption" the
"new birth in Christ Jesus." The Spirit of Christ schools us in
love, leading us out of the prison of limited and disappointing
satisfactions. The way of Christian perfection is an enlargement
of life, an ease from self-inflicted burdens, a return to oneself from
the day's defining distractions, a freedom to do good. Since our

nature itself is corrupt, true reason is a stranger to us, and so the healing of our nature is also the recovery of our reason.

Giving Up Is Hard to Do

Law puts the title of the third chapter of *Christian Perfection* in the form of a thesis: "Christianity requireth a Renunciation of the World, and all worldly Tempers" (*CP* 36). He also chooses a text that governs his lengthy treatment of renunciation. The verse is Matthew 21:45: "Whosoever he be of you that forsaketh not all that he hath, he cannot be my disciple." There is no discipleship without radical renunciation. This is a hard saying. Nevertheless, it follows directly from those "two great truths" with which Law identifies Christianity. Human beings are caught in a web of competing and consuming desires, severed from the only life that is truly able to satisfy them. The threads of this "world" bind them tightly; they are captivated by innumerable distractions and attractions. This life, which Law compares to a sleep thronged with dreams, is "at entire enmity" with God, opposed to his loving purpose, being "a state of false goods and enjoyments" (*CP* 36). Since the vehicle of this entrapment is the will, Christian life, as the process whereby God delivers us from false satisfactions, must involve thoroughgoing renunciation.

Law makes it clear that Christian perfection, along with the renunciation that it demands, is the vocation of all Christians. As such, it cannot be incompatible with marriage, family, or the diversity of occupations that Law sums up as "worldly business." The scandal of Law's exhortations is that he not only democratizes the call to perfection but also makes this "higher way" the only way: no Christian can strive for more, and no Christian may "be content with less." The vocation to perfection is inescapable.

Law takes the measure of renunciation from a truly difficult Gospel text: the story of the rich young ruler. What must I do

to inherit eternal life? Easy! Sell everything and give the proceeds to the poor. Does Law really mean this? If he does, surely
he cannot sustain his case for Christian perfection as a universal demand. No one who sells off all possessions can continue
in business or trade, estate management or farming. Yet, landowners and merchants are among the people Law is addressing,
and it is these people he commands to strive for perfection while
they manage their businesses and farm their land. "Thou must
not only keep the Commandments, *but sell that thou hast and
give to the poor*" (CP 45). The rigor of this text appeals to Law.
It is blunt and total in its demands; and it focuses upon the celebrated power of his age in this "thriving commercial nation,"
the force of those governing words, "Whosoever he be of you
that forsaketh not all that he hath, he cannot be my disciple."
Of course, there were established ways of accommodating the
text to the conditions of eighteenth-century clerical and intellectual culture, a culture generally resistant to zeal. Joseph Trapp,
bishop of Oxford and the first professor of poetry at Oxford
University, suggested that Law's governing injunction to forsake
all "may very well mean no more, than being ready to do so,
whenever the discharge of our duty shall require it."[13] The same,
therefore, would apply to selling all. We must be willing to do
so should the need — rather remote, one supposes — ever arise.
This kind of evasion infuriated Law. The author of "A Letter to
William Law," who styled himself "a Lover of Mankind," understood Christian Perfection well enough to see the importance of
the command to "sell all." He saw that Law was making the
use of riches the test case of Christian integrity. This, he fumes,
"is the main root from whence your wild extended branches
grow, that cast a noxious and baleful shade o'er all the comforts
of life."[14]

Whatever we think of Law's recommendation to "sell all," this
"main root" grows from the soil of a certain amount of common sense. Our use of money is hardly a peripheral matter; our

lives are so bound up with it that, in a commercial age, Christian faithfulness here goes a long way toward Christian faithfulness everywhere. As Law observes,

> Because the manner of using our money or spending our estate enters so far into the business of every day, and makes so great a part of our common life, that our common life must be much of the same nature as our common way of spending our estate. If reason and religion govern us in this, then reason and religion have got great hold of us. (*SC* 96)

The principal question, then, is this: What does Christian economic faithfulness look like? Is there nothing short of "Sell all and give it to the poor"? Unless Law is to abandon Christian perfection to a religious elite, he must find a form of renunciation that honors the many ties that bind men and women to secular responsibilities. He sketches this for us in the person of Miranda, who has "renounced the world to follow Christ in the exercise of humility, charity, devotion, abstinence, and heavenly affections" (*SC* 113). Miranda divides neither her life nor her money into compartments — so much for me, so much for my neighbors, so much for God. She regards all her time and substance as given in trust by God, for the use of his compassion. Miranda is just one of those who may claim their needs from her fortune. She is frugal in order to be generous. Her charity funds failing tradesmen, educates poor children and finds them employment, supports the sick and their families (*SC* 116). Law's portrait intimates that Miranda's outward charity is sustained by an inward relinquishment, the severance of personal attachment to her wealth. That she considers it as belonging to God is not merely pious phrase. Her charity, therefore, is free from self-aggrandizement; it does not bruise the recipients with their undeserved luck or dependence. No harsh word, condemning look, no sneer of superiority taints her smile; inwardly, by some strange grace, the bond of possessiveness has snapped. She does not hold it her right to grasp whatever she has as means of "self-enjoyment," but rather she receives wealth, home, health, talent, and friendships as gifts of responsibility. What is offered in all these good things is the blessed opportunity to be answerable, responsible — the gift of vocation.

A lengthy passage in the sketch of Miranda defends the practice of "indiscriminate" charity. That one should give to all who appeal, without asking questions as to their honest desert, was the controversial principle that Law adopted years later when he returned to King's Cliffe. *A Serious Call* defends Miranda's commitment to unquestioning charity with an appeal to the God who blesses "the just and the unjust" (*SC* 118). Jesus commands us to bless our enemies and teaches that God treats us according to mercy, not desert. How, then, can merit be the measure of charity? In regard to the objection that almsgiving encourages beggars: any good may be abused, but that is not a sufficient reason for not doing it. Merit certainly is a poor criterion for Christian charity, but is that sufficient to justify an indiscriminate giving? Even though circumstances rarely are clear or simple, we are responsible for giving wisely. Not all charity is wise; some does harm, some does less good and some more. To be fair to Law, charitable institutions were rare in the early eighteenth century, and those who wished to give substantially had to devise their own schemes. Perhaps, Law might argue, having no scheme is better than the dangerous prospect of judging the cases of poor men and women. His bare appeal, though, to God sending the rain on the just and the unjust alike will not do. It leaves too small a place for wisdom and knowledge, for an informed giving, for doing good with the cunning of serpents. In other words, it is too easy and evades the full risk, responsibility, and trouble of generosity. At worst, it is symptomatic of a spirituality more concerned with its own righteousness than with our neighbors' good. Nevertheless, though Law's reasons may not prove his practice, his reflections remain a challenge to our Christian integrity. After all, no less than Law's readers, I have a solid cultural stock of conventional wisdom and complacent judgment ready to ease my conscience from that reckless but thoughtful generosity that Jesus demands. Law gives us no neat recipes for devoting what we have to God. He may be a rigorist, but he is not a legalist; the way of renunciation is pursued through too many different circumstances to admit of a formula. Two insights, though, are crucial. Renunciation is the negative form of freedom. We will remain competitors, hunters in disappointment, until "we are governed by a happiness where no man can make themselves our rivals, nor prevent our attainment of it." Then it will "be no harder to help our neighbor as ourselves, than it is to wish them the enjoyment of the same light, or the same common air" (*CP* 73). This is the joy of freedom, when our hearts are weaned from their fixation upon security, status, and false satisfaction.

Law's judgment upon the world is grim: it is a prison of promises that disappoint and ruin. Perhaps that is not all we must say of the world, perhaps he misses another perspective; he would not be the first rigorist to do so. Nevertheless, his assessment is not a pious abstraction; it does open our eyes. Matilda puts all her eggs in the basket of marriageable beauty, and her daughter dies in agony from the treatment. We recognize this fashionable coercion of women's bodies, the eating disorders and ill health that follow such compulsive striving for control and conformity. Democratic societies celebrate the politics of freedom but have developed an unprecedented capacity to homogenize culture and determine our desires. If renunciation is the negative form of freedom, then, on the positive side, freedom may be described as generosity. Take the case of Mr. and Mrs. Highly Familiar. They are the reasonably conscientious Christian parents of two children; they care about doing their best, about giving the children what everyone seems to expect. Mr. Familiar is not driven by ambition but wants a reasonable standard of living, as measured by that of his colleagues and inspired somewhat by those who employ or supervise him.

Similarly, Mrs. Familiar is hardly a spendthrift; she is capable of frugality, where nobody can see it. She works hard both inside and outside the home, and she remembers fondly a time, years ago, when she traveled light and did not worry. She resents all the stuff that seems to spread out of cupboards and hang about the stairs, but she goes on buying. Money is a shifty substance that always slips away when they need it most. Mr. and Mrs. Highly Familiar worry about retirement and fear for their children should money not stretch to cover the right college. And they are in debt. The folks at the credit card companies love them; daily they calculate the interest and wait for that late payment, that underpayment, that missed payment, to apply those delicious fees that turn the screws on Mr. and Mrs. Highly Familiar.

What is the problem here? Not wasteful spending or financial fecklessness, not limited money for the kids' future, not an insufficient retirement fund or the prospect of bankruptcy: the problem is that this couple have crippled their capacity to be generous. There is just too much worry, too much debt, too many demands, too many Joneses to keep up with, to allow the freedom of generosity. Renunciation is ill-described if we think only in terms of stripping ourselves down to bare needs. Renunciation is about claiming back, dollar by dollar if necessary, the freedom to be generous. Generosity, of course, is not limited to money. We may be generous or stingy with our affection, our welcome, our compassion, our time, our God-given abilities, and so forth. Money, though, has in our day, as it had in Law's, a peculiar power, one that spreads throughout our lives. This is why Law singles it out. Other paths of generosity are inhibited by the thrall of money as we worry about it, work harder, compete more aggressively, produce more and consume more. Haunting our lives is the assumption of scarcity, that there is not enough and so we must be in competition with one another, to get as much as we can out of the little there is. Charity, government, and law step into this "war of all against all" and attempt to bring a rough peace, to regulate and ease the sorry consequences. At this point, if we take the gospel seriously, as Law suggests, we unmask the assumption of scarcity for what it is: a denial of God. Creation is the work of generosity, and God gives himself unstintingly as he creates, redeems, and raises from the dead. We live, therefore, within the horizon of plenty, of an inexhaustible life, and so we may be generous, as is "our heavenly Father." Christian generosity is a sacrament of hope for folk weary under the dark belief that there will never be enough.

One of Law's critics challenged him with an appeal to God's "good creation." God has provided us with much that gives us enjoyment, not to mention the very capacity for experiencing pleasure. Law, however, has turned up the heat of the gospel's demands to such a pitch as to refuse those divine benefits that are "the innocent pleasures of life." Does Law have any place for the "innocent pleasures of life"? He certainly expects a strict accounting of time. The Christian "truly knows why he should spend any time well, knows that it is never allowable to throw any time away" (*SC* 92). The largest constituency among Law's intended readership was precisely the class that had time to waste, those who lived "at leisure," with a control over their time scarcely imaginable to most of us today. However, Law's demand that hours as well as fortune be accounted for is not restricted to that class. The idea of any time, anywhere, that is not put to some useful purpose makes him seethe: "To talk... of *spare time* is to talk of *something* that never did nor ever will belong to any Christian" (*CP* 168). At this point, we are likely to feel sympathy with the defender of "innocent pleasures," so caution is needed in assessing this aspect of Law's teaching. Undoubtedly, Christian exhortations to the stewardship of time contributed to the pressure that modern Western culture has placed upon the use of time. We have absorbed time into economics: we spend time, waste time, buy time, and live on borrowed time. The importance of time for leisure, even for "spirituality," is now widely touted but often still justified as ultimately productive of a higher over-all efficiency in the use of time. Whatever contribution Christian teaching has made to this bondage to productive time, though, the secularized version is vastly more burdensome. Law may require us to be strictly accountable for the way we spend our days, but this included contemplation and quiet, study and reflection, social action, and the maintenance of extensive and varied social bonds. It was not dangerously narrowed toward economic productivity and consumption. That said, however, there remains a strong drive in *A Serious Call* toward judging everything in terms of "purposefulness." We might argue in response that a life that glorifies God should not only be purposeful in many of the ways approved by Law but also have room for the "purposeless." Christianity inherited the practice of the Sabbath from Judaism and, in doing so, inherited a symbol for "purposeless" joy. Sabbath rest is not purposeful in the sense that it merely prepares us to get back to work again. The Sabbath is the anticipation of eternal life, when all tears are dried and the bruises of all labor healed forever. Are we to think that on this point, at least, Law's critics were entirely right? No, because they had matters backward in assuming a *right* to pleasure. Circumstances have so arranged themselves that Christians are now wealthy, free from persecution, and with time to spare on the good things of life. This is a given, and the business of Christian duty and devotion is to fit round it as much as possible. Law's argument is quite the reverse. He clearly does not like the word *pleasure*. It has, perhaps, something of the same chilling resonance for him that the word *fun* has gathered for me after raising three teenage children. If he does have a place for enjoyment — and surely someone remembered for playing with children must — the experience of delight, and what gives delight, is set within the terms of devotion and not prior to them.[15]

This is precisely what we find in some important, if easily missed, references in *A Serious Call*. Devotion is not an end in itself; it is the means by which we "partake of the divine nature." This does not eliminate joy from life but rather creates new joys out of an intense engagement, what Law calls "strong satisfactions" (*SC* 148). From the outside, the uncompromised commitment that God demands appears severe and harsh. But from the midst of the self-giving that constitutes the holy life, Law's testimony is that "it creates new comforts in everything that we do," and by thus losing ourselves, we "heighten and increase all that is happy and comfortable in human life" (*SC* 159, 148).

Chapter 3 _____

Devout and Holy...and Reasonable?

"'Let Newton Be!' and All Was Light"

In 1739, Joseph Trapp published *The Nature, Folly, Sin, and Danger of Being Righteous Overmuch*, a vigorous and rather pompous attack on William Law, John Wesley, and George Whitefield. The title may seem peculiar coming from a bishop, but Trapp is referring to what he considers excessive forms of piety and devotion. His examples include charity when one is unable to provide for one's family, extremes of fasting, and an undue, self-righteous abstinence. We can avoid all this disruptive nonsense as soon as we realize that righteousness is the mean, the point of balance between unrighteousness on the one hand and "over-righteousness" on the other. Trapp's Christianity is moderate, a sensible accommodation to the better opinions and practices of the age. This is easy to mock, but sober, commonsensical, moderate clergy did much good in the eighteenth century and, keeping company with the great and powerful, probably did prevent a fair amount of ill. Trapp, however, does not frame faith and life with that eschatological urgency characteristic of William Law. His Jesus is not the coming one so much as the one who has already come and now returned to heaven. The bishop does not face us with the voracious demands of God and the all-consuming, all-expecting relationship that he offers. We have seen what Trapp made of the rich young ruler, but those equally troubling sayings in the Sermon on the Mount — the commands to turn the other cheek, to love enemies — those, too, he politely turns away.

> [They] are only proverbial and hyperbolical phrases, pro-
> hibiting revenge, and a litigious temper; commanding a
> patient enduring of injuries, in lesser matters, or when they
> are in any degree tolerable, according to the dictates of sober,
> reason, prudence, and equity.[1]

There is nothing wrong with Jesus except a regrettable tendency to exaggerate. Along with this comfortable moderation of
Jesus' teaching, though, evaporates Law's realism about evil, his
recognition of God's holiness, and the extravagant promise of
salvation.

Trapp's weakness as an exegete and, as Law pointed out in a
published reply, his failure to clarify what he thought was righteous enough do not, however, blunt the point of his questions.
Are Law's exhortations reasonable? Are they practical or just
impossibly grueling? These questions persist even if we are convinced that Law does not set his face against all enjoyment. We
will pursue them in turn, the first because Law refers to reason
constantly in *A Serious Call,* and we need to know what he meant
by it. Then, in the next chapter, we will turn to Law's practical
advice, to his description of the devout life, and consider it as the
practice of the possible.

To call the eighteenth century the "Age of Reason" is asking for trouble. A society with an appallingly cumbersome legal
system, which offered little personal security to its members, in
which small girls were hanged for trifles and women burned alive
for murdering their husbands, where pelting foreign visitors, especially the French, was common sport, and mob violence fairly
routine is hardly an example of rationality, or if it is, it does
not say much for reason. Nevertheless, however much the English, even the wealthy and well-educated, loved fighting, swearing,
drinking to great excess, public floggings, and dunking Methodists, they also loved "Reason." "Reason" is, perhaps, the most
celebrated and lauded idea of the time, particularly during the

early decades of the century.[2] Rationality was God's greatest gift to human beings, while "enthusiasm," or claims to supernatural inspirations and guidance, was one of the devil's worst temptations. The "poison of Enthusiasm," George Hickes warned the University of Oxford, would reduce Christianity to "the most wild, uncertain, and unintelligible institution that ever was in the world." True Christianity goes hand in hand with reason. Christianity has, argued Archbishop Tillotson, "hardly imposed any laws upon us...but what every man's reason either dictates to him to be necessary, or approves as highly fit and reasonable." Christianity's critics, on other hand, put it to the same bar of reason and found it false. Either way, reason was the touchstone. By reason, we perceive "the truth, falsehood, probability or improbability of propositions"; the rules of reason are the "laws of God," and, as some bolder folk went on to claim, reason "is the only foundation of all certitude." Writers not only celebrated reason because we have it now, but also they dreamed of reason's future, of fully rational societies where religious and political squabbling was unknown. Since "no mathematical truth is clearer than the conviction that man is essentially a rational agent," the human future lies in reason and reasonable religion.

The hopes placed in reason's capacity to solve human problems, overcome social divisions, and create a prosperous society were partly funded by a crisis of confidence in traditional authorities, particularly the Bible and the church. During the middle years of the seventeenth century, the English had fought one another in civil war, executed a monarch, abolished the established church, and undergone years of social and economic turmoil. For a later generation, the period became a byword for religious disputatiousness and mutual intolerance, for the spawning of sects, for outrageous claims to possess the Spirit or speak up for God, and for inspired crazies who went "naked for a sign" or announced that Christ's coming needed only a little help from them. England remained, of course, a Christian, scriptural, and churchly culture, but older ways of securing ecclesiastical authority or appealing to biblical truths had lost face. Reason, perhaps, might point the way to peace and ground Christian belief and practice in a way uniting all people of goodwill.

New discoveries, too, funded reason's status. The Royal Society for the Improvement of Natural Knowledge received its charter in 1662 and in the following decades boasted Robert Boyle and Isaac Newton among an intellectually star-studded membership. Introducing the first history of the society in 1667, Thomas Sprat wondered

> what can be more delightful for an Englishman to consider, that notwithstanding all the late miseries of his country; it has been able in a short time so well to recover itself: . . . [as] to set on foot, a new way of improvement of Arts, as great and beneficial . . . as any the wittiest and happiest age has ever invented.[3]

The new developments in science and mathematics flooded light into what had appeared intractably obscure. The world, though daily as unpredictable and dangerous as ever, was being resolved into order, with all the promise of regularity and law. Newton and company had lifted the curtain around Nature and seen the pulleys and wheels that kept it going.

A better Troop she [Nature] ne're together drew. Methinks, like Gideon's little Band, God with Design has pickt out you, To do these noble Wonders by a Few . . .

> New Scenes of Heaven already we espy, . . .
> Natures great Workes no distance can obscure,
> No smalness her near Objects can secure
> Y' have taught the curious Sight to press
> Into the privatest recess
> Of her imperceptible Littleness.[4]

As for the great Sir Isaac,

> The heavens are all his own; from the wild rule
> Of whirling Vortices, and circling Spheres,
> To their first great simplicity restored.
> The schools astonish'd stood; but found it vain
> To combat still with demonstration strong....
> At once their pleasing visions fled,
> With the gay shadows of the morning mix'd,
> When Newton rose, our philosophic sun![5]

The art of science is to see things clear, shed light into darkness, and resolve contradictions and complexity into "their first great simplicity." Dreams and fables might have amused humanity, whiled away its time, but now the "blaze of truth" was here to set us straight. Given the heady promise of all this, it is hardly surprising that reason would seem the way to bring the same order, the same agreement, into religion.

Law refers to the human capacity for "reason" almost one hundred and forty times in *A Serious Call*; clearly, he has absorbed this cultural emphasis and shares to some degree his contemporaries' investment in rationality. He tells us solemnly that it is "our strict duty to live by reason" and "absolutely necessary" to order our lives by "rules of reason and piety" (*SC* 48, 77). The book concludes with the reminder that "reason is our universal law, that obliges us in all places, and at all times" (*SC* 351). More tellingly, the value that Law places upon reason informs the strategies by which he seeks to persuade his readers. Again and again, he sets up arguments that issue in what appears a simple choice between rationality and irrationality. If we are always humble and reverent in prayer, is that not more important than the occasional vanity in our appearance or pride in our hard work? Of course not, Law replies:

> If we could suppose that God rejects pride in our prayers
> and alms but bears with pride in our dress, our persons, or

estates, it would be the same thing as to suppose that God condemns falsehood in some actions, but allows it in others.

(SC 84–85)

Law focuses the familiar, ambiguous conditions of our lives through images that make judgment upon them seem utterly straightforward. Ambition drives us, we are troubled by the elusiveness of success and cut with a thousand small disappointments, but is this not just life, the way things are? No, says Law, your case is as a man "passing his days in disquiet because he could not walk upon the water or catch birds as they fly by him." We are anxious because we pursue what is no more our "proper good than walking upon the water or catching birds" (*SC* 150–51).

Eighteenth-century passion for reason was routinely accompanied by invocations of light and order, the blessings of clarity and security. Thus, outrageously, by Alexander Pope:

> Nature and Nature's Laws lay hid in Night;
> God said, *Let Newton be!* and all was Light.[6]

A Serious Call, too, is permeated by implicit and explicit appeals to light and order. Law strips his arguments of any obscurity, repeats and reinforces them in varying forms, often announcing his desire to put matters "in the clearest light." Style, argument, character sketch, wit, and metaphor are devices to make matters "plain." The worldly person is like one who "puts out his eyes, rather than enjoy the light." The lazy, who sleep through the morning, are "shut up in sleep and darkness," and harmful passions "blind and darken" the mind. Law also believes strongly in the ordering power of rules, of the progress to be made through simple and regular practices. A rule grants power over, and order within, an unruly and disordered self. Law's references to light and his confidence in rules mark his share in the age's reverence for reason. As we might expect, though, closer inspection will find

Law putting reason to unconventional ends. A common valuation of reason funds an uncommon account of Christianity. There is a rigorist wolf inside this fashionable sheep's clothing.

Despite the widespread agreement that reason was a jolly good thing, there was surprisingly little contemporary discussion about the precise meaning of "reason." A good approach, therefore, is to start not with definitions but rather with practice. How does Law employ the term? Law understands "reason" in three rather different senses. Reason is, first, the power to choose with understanding; it makes the difference between blind instinct and human will. Since we are rational, we are able to identify ends and devise means to secure them. Reason is the "instrument" for doing this, and, like any other instrument, it may be used well or ill. We may and do reason "ourselves into all sorts of follies."[7] Always operative in choice, reason is also the power to follow an argument and spot the true from the false. Reason sorts out implications, recognizes demonstrations or proof, gauges probabilities, and exposes contradictions. The fall may have played havoc with our capacity to choose and stick to what is truly good for us, but still we are able to discern true arguments from false even if we fortify ourselves against doing so. Law's whole approach assumes this rational capacity. Finally, there is a more theologically loaded use. Our vocation is to live according to reason, not just in the instrumental sense, which we cannot help doing, but as those who fulfill the conditions of creation, the reason of our being, the divine purpose given with our nature. If we use our reason truly, we will see light because "reason" in us is the capacity to see "reason" in everything: to see the way things are, how they hang together, and, more particularly, to recognize the world and ourselves as God's creation. This, of course, is reason's true vocation; and the human tragedy is that for "reasoning well," as Law puts it, for godly reasoning, sin has crippled us.

While "reason," then, is a decidedly positive term for Law, at least at this stage of his career, he is none too blithe about rational enquiry and reflection in a world of skewed desires and intricate self-deception. This was not, in itself, a controversial position; the conviction that respect for reason should be bounded by a critical self-awareness was widely shared. Not only is reason, more frequently than we like to think, the slave of our passions, but also it finds an essential boundary in the knowledge of God. The poet Abraham Cowley appeals to reason, "which (God be prais'd!) still Walks, for all / It's old Original Fall," as a necessary guide to Scripture. However, if we must be grateful that "mysteries Divine / May with our Reason joyn," we must also remember that, though reason may lead us to truth, it "cannot through Faiths Myst'eries see."[8] Cowley's poem, however, is not untypical in intimating that the enthusiasm lies with reason while acknowledgment of its limits is a rather perfunctory nod to theological convention. Not surprisingly, then, there were those eager to rip off even this fig leaf to sport in the utopia of reason.

Reason before Mystery

Among the enthusiastic rationalists was Matthew Tindal, against whom Law published his best polemical work, *The Case of Reason; or, Natural Religion, Fairly and Fully Stated*. Published in 1731, this work attacked, in brief and lively compass, Tindal's plodding, repetitious, though certainly controversial, book *Christianity as Old as the Creation; or, the Gospel a Republication of the Religion of Nature*. Tindal was a fairly extreme representative of the conviction that reason could sort out the ambiguities of religion as it had our knowledge of the natural world. Whatever Christians may have said for the past eighteen hundred years, Tindal assures us, God has revealed nothing more than what sober, reasonable reflection on nature might have told them all along. He writes with an oily, smug sense of the ease with which Christian faith may be shown to boil down to a "republication" of "natural religion."

> By *Natural Religion*, I understand the belief of the existence
> of a God, and the sense and practice of those duties which
> result from the knowledge we, by our reason, have of him
> and his perfections; and of ourselves, and our own imper-
> fections; and of the relation we stand to him and our fellow
> creatures: so that the Religion of Nature takes in everything
> that is founded on the reason and nature of things.[9]

All you need is here. Away with all the obfuscations, the dreary
controversies, the theological backbiting that accompanies doctrines of Trinity, incarnation, atonement. All these are tricks to
befuddle you, obscurities to keep theologians in jobs. If we just
use our reason, if we observe the world around us and keep our
thoughts steady, then the fog of mystery will lift and everything
become as clear as daylight.

Law begins his systematic mauling of Tindal's work by summarizing the Deist's main claims. Simply put, Tindal argues that
human reason is our only means of acquiring knowledge of God,
and that any kind of special revelation to particular people at
particular times would be unworthy of a rational God. We may,
therefore, be quite confident in the sufficiency of our reason to discover all that we need to know about the Almighty and about the
blessings and responsibilities of our relationship with him. Rather
than peppering Tindal with appeals to Scripture, Law proceeds by
showing that the Deist argument proves the reverse of the Deist
case. We know God and discern his will, Tindal claims, by attending carefully to ourselves and our needs, as well as to Nature
and our particular circumstances. God's action and God's will are
governed by whatever is fitting given "the nature of things, and
the relation they have to one another."[10] Very well, Law responds,
"I readily grant, that the nature, reason, and relations of things
and persons, and the fitness of actions resulting from thence, is
the *sole rule* of God's actions."[11] This principle, however, points
in a direction most embarrassing to the Deist.

If we act correctly when we respect the nature of things and persons, then the fitness of God's actions must be founded in "his own *divinely perfect* and *incomprehensible* nature."[12] God, surely, must act consistently with his own nature. God's own being, however, is incomprehensible, utterly beyond finite fathoming. The measure of God's actions must, therefore, be, in principle, *above* all human comprehension. God might, of course, choose to act according to the fitness of things as viewed and understood from our perspective — as an adult might choose, perversely, to act from the perspective of a child — but to do so would make him the one thing that Tindal utterly rejects: an *arbitrary* God. After all, there could be no good reason for infinite wisdom and goodness to act according to the lights of a finite wisdom and a goodness spoiled by sin. Since God is not arbitrary, he always acts according to his "incomprehensible perfections." How, then, can finite reason measure the immeasurable?

Tindal, though, does think that God acts according to standards derivable from human reason. At our best, when we are thinking straight, we share the same perspective as God for deciding what is good and what is not, and for figuring out the meaning of creation. Tindal is quite shameless in this elevation of human reason: "We may contemplate the great dignity of our rational nature, since our reason for kind, though not for degree, is of the same nature with God's."[13] The root difference between Law and Tindal is theological. They are not talking about the same God. If Tindal's work is anything to go by, then a smug insistence on the omnicompetence of human reason ends up with a rather limited view of God. God's reason and ours are different, but only by degree rather than in kind. Our reason is ordered toward the finite, it is expressed in language, and it proceeds by steps from one conclusion to another. Our reason follows arguments, puts ideas together, constructs cases, concludes from evidence, makes inferences, deduces. Tindal seems to suggest that God does much the same thing, only he does it faster, more accurately, and gets it right. God is a mind alongside other minds, only a lot smarter. Tindal also tells us that God obeys the rules of reason. His decisions are founded on it, and ours should be. By saying that, though, Tindal places God and humankind together under a system of law that binds and is greater than them both. God obeys laws. Tindal defends this rather indignantly:

> If there is nothing right or wrong, good or bad, antecedently and independently of the will of God, there can then be no reason, why God should will, or command one thing, rather than another.[14]

And, of course, we cannot have that, for it would make God "arbitrary."

Tindal has given us a domesticated God. However powerful and terrifically brainy this God might be, he is one entity among others, albeit the most important. God is not the immeasurable ground of the system of being; rather, he is part of it. That, however, is precisely what Law rejects. Whenever we are dealing with God, he tells us, incomprehensibility, the bowing of language and thought before the inexpressible, is inescapable. God is not one object alongside others; he is not even the most important being among all beings. God is not "one of" anything. God is the utterly unique giver of existence, transcending all creatures, everything that receives being as a gift from his hand. He is not part of the system to which our reason is ordered, and so he is not at the disposal of our reason. He is irreducibly, incalculably different. However strenuous our thought and subtle our concepts, God remains mysterious. To use a much misunderstood but classical term, God is "mystery."

This, however, was not something that one said in front of a Deist. "Mystery" summed up all that was wrong with religion. One of the earliest blasts of Deist polemic was John Toland's *Christianity Not Mysterious; or, A Treatise Shewing That There Is Nothing in the Gospel Contrary to Reason, nor above It: and*

That No Christian Doctrine Can Be Properly Call'd a Mystery.[15]
"Mystery" was what priests and theologians dreamed up to keep us from thinking for ourselves. So, when priests wanted to stop us from thinking, they cried, "It is a mystery!" A mystery was an illegitimate, ecclesiastical roadblock on reason's modern freeway. All this fury, though, rather missed the point. As Toland's book title suggests, he and similar critics fastened onto "mystery" as referring to doctrines rather than, first and foremost, to the God about whom those doctrines teach. They suggest that a mystery is something that, with more effort, more information, and less priestcraft, we could solve, illuminate, and clear up. Should we be unable to think a so-called mystery through to our satisfaction, if we had to live with mystery, then, in the Deist view, human dignity would deflate in the terrible defeat of human reason.

I tell my wife that my lifelong inability to eat without smearing food on myself is a mystery. It is not, though. A team of psychologists, sociologists, experts in anatomy, and arbiters of etiquette would, I am sure, have little trouble in sounding my problem to the depths and leaving me in no doubt as to some humiliating explanation. My perennial muckiness is no mystery. For all that we do not know, for all that eludes our understanding and, perhaps, forever will, nothing created can be said, in and of itself, to be a "mystery." Only God is properly named "mystery," and if mystery turns out to be inherent in all reality, it does so because reality is God's creation. To recognize God as "mystery" is to confess him as the One who establishes the coordinates of finitude and who, as their Creator, lies always beyond them. There is no comprehending the limitless, no measuring the immeasurable, no "getting to the bottom" of the inexhaustible. However, when this eternally, necessarily mysterious God reveals himself to us, we find that "knowing" this unknowable God is not the frustration of the human thirst to know but rather is its fulfillment. When the mind recognizes that God is truly incomprehensible, it does not slam into a brick wall; it comes home, rejoicing in the endless light that enlightens everything.

In all God's mighty works, in giving being and restoring broken existences to his own abundance, God acts according to "his own *divinely perfect* and *incomprehensible* nature." There is nothing, therefore, without mystery. The tiniest inhabitant of the merest drop of water, the largest of cosmic suns, and all things between, bear their witness to mystery, to the God who made them. As Law puts it, "We must be surrounded with mystery for this very reason, because God acts by a certain rule, his own nature." This has very important implications. If we let him, God teaches us to read. The Holy Spirit illumines and opens both the Scriptures and what, in Law's day, was often referred to as the "Book of Nature." Learning to read the latter, "in the Spirit," we discover "Nature" as *creation.* We know the world as a complex field of signs, signifying this mysterious God. Created signs never, of course, capture the mystery — God always exceeds them — but they bear witness nevertheless, sometimes clearly, often enigmatically, sometimes darkly.

If everything comes from and returns, in life and longing, to mystery, then everything is more than it seems. If all things find their meaning in the incomprehensible God, as expressions of his loving purpose, then the meaning of every created thing is unfathomable and all our ideas about each and every creature are merely provisional. Since there is nothing that is not a gift and nothing that does not find its meaning hidden in the love of the Giver, then nothing is just what it appears to be. If God is "mystery" and not the projection of our limited reason, then we are summoned to wonder and to care for his creation, to engage it with tact, respect, and a loving caution. There is more to it than meets the eye, or, for that matter, more than meets the analysis of any science. Within everything, the presence of the Giver is concealed.

Modern culture has established something of an industry in defining us, in telling us what human beings are all about. Social scientists, economists, evolutionary biologists, and psychologists have contributed enormously to our knowledge of human beings. Secular sciences, however, are concerned with objectifying human beings, rendering them as calculable elements within systems of explanation. They have fostered strong reductionist tendencies: approaches to human beings as "nothing but" complicated animals, or economic units, or clusters of psychological drives, or patterns of stimulus and response. Such accounts of our humanity have all too easily justified treating persons as things: from the cynical orchestration of individuals as "consumers" to the ghastly construction of death camps in the name of social evolution and racial purity or proletarian revolution and the forward movement of history.

If human beings, however, participate in the mystery of God, then they are never "nothing but . . . " and their worth is weighed by the holiness of the Giver. Put more personally, reverence for God as the Mysterious Giver in every gift of being is what will keep us from taking our loved ones and our neighbors for granted, from the stultifying arrogance that assumes that we have got them pegged. Finally, we may add, if mystery is inescapable and we are always being called beyond what we can *think* to what is known only in being loved, then we might reconsider our culture's tendency to oppose and privilege reason over other forms of knowing: emotional, intuitive, aesthetic. Not surprisingly, Tindal assures us, "the Holy Ghost cannot deal with men as rational creatures, but by *proposing arguments* to convince their understanding and influence their wills, in the same manner as if proposed by other agents."[16] Really?

This discussion of reason may seem to have carried us a long way from Law's practical treatises. It has turned up something important, though. We noticed much earlier that Law's account of the Christian life is an uncompromising one: Give everything! Sell it all! Renounce the world! Now we can see the driving force behind such insistence. The God whom Law confesses is the utterly unique One, who cannot be contained within the reach of our reason. Tindal is quite confident that God "can require nothing of us, but what makes for our happiness."[17] He also thinks that, given our rational capacities, we are quite capable of judging what that happiness is and how to get it. Tindal's God issues no call that goes beyond a sober assessment of what is sensible, nor does he offer to give the power to perform what exceeds our courage, nor does he promise a fulfillment beyond our imaginings. As we saw, Law is more than happy to acknowledge that reason serves us in essential ways. He appeals to it, even suggests that we are lost without it. When, however, we reason ourselves into a God whose ways are our ways and who demands only what we would set ourselves, then reason has betrayed us and points only to our plight as sinners. Law thus remembers the God who puts aged Abraham to wandering, appoints Moses to threaten a Pharaoh, and sends the Son of Man to Golgotha, none of which seemed calculated to increase their happiness. On the strength of such a cloud of witnesses, Law reads the New Testament and finds for us a most scary calling. This, however, makes John Wesley's question, which we raised in the last chapter, more urgent than ever. Has Law forgotten grace? Are we to wear ourselves out in striving and still have no certainty of mercy? Is this all law and no gospel? To see whether there is any substance in Wesley's accusation, we will look at Law's description of a day in the "devout and holy life." What form does it take, and what sustains it?

_____

Chapter 4

A Devout and Holy Day

Strategies of Formation

One may be unreasonable without being irrational. Dr. Trapp thought that "being righteous overmuch" was not only unchristian but also "contrary to reason." However "over-righteous," though, Law was not, in Trapp's view, crazy, unable to argue in a straight line, or likely to insist that the world was flat. Rather, Law was immoderate, made excessive demands, lacked sobriety, turned pebbles of weakness into boulder-sized sins. He was, in short, unreasonable. In moral and religious matters, especially, this aspect of reason was never far away for Law's contemporaries. On the one hand, reason preserved us from falsehood; on the other hand, it kept us moderate. Reason's dictates, as Trapp assures us, are "sober." If Christianity was a "reasonable" religion — and many who were a long way from being Deists thought that it was — then its doctrines were plain, sensible, and soundly based. So were its demands. Belief in God was reasonable, and the God believed in was also reasonable in his expectations. They were not burdensome, overstrenuous, or immoderate. We have seen what Law thought of moderation. "Moderation" is the excuse for comfy complacency; it is Christianity without tears. Once we know whom we are talking about when we say "God," reason, in Law's view, backs precisely what Dr. Trapp believes unreasonable: the pressing demands of the Sermon on the Mount, of the voice from the Mosaic cloud, of the Messianic "Take up your cross."

Law has no time for this reasonable Christianity, with its moderation, yet *A Serious Call* manages to make the devout and holy life appear surprisingly attractive, even accessible. It is demanding but not daunting or dispiriting. At its best, Law's is an exhilarating description of the dedicated, self-aware Christian life. Much of this has to do with the tone of the book, which, though frequently urgent, consistently suggests a sense of the possible, of a life waiting to be ventured. This tone of confidence is conveyed by Law's appeals to straightforward reasoning, by the forcefulness of his arguments, the clarity of the practical suggestions, and the vividness of his character sketches. He drives the reader to believe that she is just a step from discovering "how little is lost and how much gained...by a strict and exact piety" (*SC* 185).

It is important to ask where this tone comes from. After all, we are talking about a *holy* life, about Christian *perfection*, and surely this cannot boil down to a series of manageable proposals that need only our perseverance to succeed? Perhaps the culture is speaking here, louder than his theology, and Law is caught up into the optimism, that sense of human potential, which is at least one aspect of eighteenth-century English culture. Do we have here that energy for education in which so many of Law's contemporaries put their faith? Or the trust in systematic application, orderliness, and method that inspired so many, from John Wesley and the Holy Club, who were pious by exact rule, to Dr. John Freke's methodical attempts to expose the fiery life force by dubious experiments with cats and candles? Law undoubtedly was confident in education, even progressive in his bold assertion that differences in attainment between men and women were purely consequent on differences in their education. Were women to receive a man's education in science and arts, Law predicts, "I have much suspicion that they would often prove our superiors" (*SC* 262). As to rule and method, Law thinks that nothing can be accomplished without it and, it appears, almost everything with it. "He that has begun to live by rule, has gone a great way towards the perfection of his life" (*SC* 111). Law shares with many of his contemporaries, too, an optimism regarding introspection. Careful self-observation will bring a steady light into our hearts, judging our progress, exposing our motives, and testing our integrity. Ideas of unconscious motivation, of our vigor in self-deception, and of the frailty with which we are judges in our case do not cloud this happy assurance. Is it then the case that when it came down to practice, the sunny side of Law broke through and the genial aspect of his culture came to the fore?

This would be an unwise conclusion, despite Law's genuine faith in education, rule, method, and self-examination. Between our psychological aptitude for rules, any gift we may naturally possess for introspection, any worldly curriculum, and the "new state of things" that is the life of a Christian there is fixed a great gulf. Even the most respectable sinner is an alien in that land of wakefulness upon which the eyes of faith open. No amount of moral shoe-shining can heal the human condition, as Law understands it. Not only have we run up a remarkable tab of selfish and destructive actions, but also we exist in a condition of "deplorable corruption." We cannot act our way out of this any more than whiten a wall with black paint. Something, then, must stand between Law's stern grip on human sinfulness and the encouraging tone of his exhortations, something that John Wesley missed. If Law's vigorous "wake-up call" is, in the end, not disheartening but hopeful, then behind it there must be more than solid effort and methodical practice. Does it appear if we attend to Law's description of the practice of a holy day?

In the second half of *A Serious Call* Law maps out a day's devotion. He divides the days according to times of prayer and proposes a particular theme to shape and guide our prayer on each occasion. Law's readers would have found this a fairly familiar strategy. Of course, the practice of praying at set times of the day is ancient and, in Christianity, most notably provided the liturgical pulse of monastic life. Protestant devotional texts, however, took up the idea in a form modified for a lay spirituality. Lewis Bayly's *The Practice of Piety, Directing a Christian How to Walk That He May Please God* provided a short guide to Christian belief, a scheme for reading the Bible, instructions on aspects of Christian life such as one's duties to the church and how to prepare for the Sabbath. Bayly also has prayers and meditations for both morning and evening, graces for meals, and devotions for bedtime.[1] Published at least as early as 1612, Bayly's work had gone into over fifty editions by the time Law was writing *A Serious Call*. A slightly earlier work, Henry Bull's *Christian Praiers and Holie Meditations*, equips the Christian reader, in addition to morning and evening prayers, with "cogitations for about the midday," and with prayers for times such as "when you go forth of the doors" and "when the candles be lit." There is even a prayer for "when you feel sleep to be coming," which, as one would need to wake up to read it, might make for a long night.[2]

A Serious Call is not, like these devotional books, a manual of prayers; it is not designed to be kept at hand and *used* as was *The Practice of Piety*. The purpose is to exhort, to expound the rationale of Christian devotion, and to offer prescriptions for practice. Also, *A Serious Call* addresses a less general readership, a constituency of those whose time is more at their disposal. For the most part, Law describes devotions for the life that he himself lived, a life that was the privilege of England's gentry and landowning class and of those, like Law, with independent means. The principles of *A Serious Call* do indeed apply far more widely, and Law emphasizes intention rather than the particular shape of execution, but his setting aside five times of the day for prayer does reflect the looser constraints enjoyed by "people of leisure . . . who are forced into poor contrivances, idle visits, and ridiculous diversions, merely to get rid of hours that hang heavily upon their hands" (*SC* 202).

In ordering the day as he has, Law intends a recovery of the model of "primitive Christianity." Even though prayer at specific times is not expressly commanded by Scripture, we know, he insists, that this was the apostolic practice, and we cannot go wrong by emulating it. To underline the early Christian foundations of this regular prayer, Law introduces the practice with a reference to the "biblical" reckoning of time. We settle to pray at the third, sixth, ninth, and twelfth hours of the day, that is, at 9:00 a.m., 12:00 noon, 3:00 p.m., and 6:00 p.m. To these hours, Law adds prayer first thing in the morning, immediately after we get up. This needs no special justification, as "I take it for granted, that every Christian, that is in health, is up early in the morning."

After all, he explains, having business with God in prayer is immeasurably more important than any worldly duty, and so, since we rise for the one, we should delay the other still less. Not surprisingly, Law indulges in some stern finger-wagging at those who lie abed "shut up in sleep and darkness" (*SC* 189). To our first prayers, Law attaches the theme of praise and thanksgiving and considers the use of psalms and songs as aids to devotion. When we return to our knees at 9:00 a.m., we consider humility and all that fosters this primary virtue. Then, at noon, the subject of prayer is "universal love," intercession being the way that love is expressed in prayer. Devotion at midafternoon reinforces our acceptance of God's will, and at 6:00 p.m., looking back over our day, we turn to repentance and confession.

A Serious Call divides, then, into two major sections. The first thirteen chapters tell us why the devout life is a necessity and how holiness is our true happiness. They also provide examples of Christian duties, of the actions of a holy life. Then, beginning in chapter 14, Law turns to prayer in an extended account of a day's devotion that takes us to the book's final, summarizing chapter. This structure embodies a very ancient distinction between the "active" life and the "contemplative" life. In the spiritually democratizing context of Law's Protestantism, the outward way of service and the inward way of prayer are integrated within a spirituality for lay life in the world. A traditional note is struck, though, in that the argument ascends to the topic of prayer after discussion of the "active" life. This is quite appropriate, as prayer is the "the nearest approach to God, and the highest enjoyment of Him, that we are capable of in this life." Intent on God, our hearts opened in gratitude, our wills stretched toward the good that we find so scary and hard, then, "we are in our highest state...the utmost heights of human greatness" (*SC* 190).

The division of the book is suggestive in another way, though. Law cannot tackle prayer at the beginning because of the central misunderstanding that he wants to correct. We often think of our lives as divided into different spheres of concern, such as work, family, leisure. Despite the way we often manage matters, though, God does not show up on this map, corralled into a sphere named "religion." Prayer is not the religious business that satisfies God, so that we can get on with the rest of our lives on our own time. "Julius is very fearful of missing prayers," and yet if he "was to read all the New Testament from the beginning to the end, he would find his course of life condemned in every page of it" (*SC* 49). Holiness knows no sphere that is not God's, no moment that is not his gift, no relationship that is not his charge, no breath that is not from his pleasure. Until we understand this, we will misunderstand prayer. Prayer is the most important thing we do, the "most exalted use of our best faculties," but *only* insofar as it is not just one more thing that we do — the "God-activity" to be checked off alongside all our other activities. Prayer is this "highest" employment precisely as the center of a whole life offered, a life in which the internal borders and checkpoints, the barriers to God's interest are being abandoned. *A Serious Call* leads us through the active life first because we can take the measure of prayer only when we have understood the measure of God's claim. Then these times of prayer, to which Law devotes the second half of the book, open up as the form of our intimacy with God, the reconciled conversation that shapes our will and sustains our actions in hope. Law orders his regimen of prayer to disclose the structural elements, the sustaining girders of this relationship: the actions of praise, intercession, and confession, and the primary dispositions of humility and acceptance of God's will.

The "devout and holy life," then, does not consist in isolated, compartmentalized moments; rather, it is a set of the heart that finds varied but consistent expression. This requires that the practices of devotion are "habitual." There should be both an openness to growth and a stability of direction. Law's prescription certainly is for a demanding life, but not one of perpetual strain; there is struggle but within an underlying steadiness, a peace and sure-footedness mediated by the rhythms of actions and attitudes that have become habitual. Law insists, of course, that God looks upon the heart, that his measure is intention, not the action as such. Nevertheless, intention without practice is false, just as practice without intention is empty. So Law takes forms very seriously. Getting up early for prayer, deciding upon set times for thanksgiving, intercession, and repentance, dedicating a particular place in the house or a corner of a room, taking an appropriate posture, using certain prayers regularly — these articulations we cannot do without. Forms like these are the scaffolding of habit, and just as what we do expresses what we love, so what we determine to do — and do regularly — can kindle, order, and sustain our love.

In prayer, we tell the truth about ourselves. As God gives us freedom, we speak honestly and without dissembling. We do not need to hide changes in our mood or our energy. If prayer is regular, then certainly we will not always "feel like it." We may be angry or resentful, dejected or distracted, worried or grieving. We may be tired or sick. The stability resides in the practice and the faithfulness of God, not in our mood-blown, eventful lives. So we must be frank about our condition and, when we are low, take to more set prayers, use psalms appropriate to our condition, be content with simple statements of our need. In this way, change becomes the *material* of prayer; the joyous and the wretched in our experience are received into the same ark that God has provided for us. "Devotion will be made doubly beneficial to us, when it watches to receive and sanctify all these changes of our state" (*SC* 201). Truthfulness is found not only in what we say and acknowledge before God but also in the practice of prayer itself. Here, there are two false extremes. Obsessive attention to outward forms leads to superstition as the forms themselves cease to be media and become obstacles to fellowship with God. On the other hand, that spiritual snootiness that will have no such helps risks collapsing into an illusory paradise of fuzzy feelings as it resolves "all religion into a quietism or mystic intercourses with God in silence" (*SC* 216). Prayer should rather express the truth about God's making of us, that "we are neither all soul or all body" (*SC* 216). "The soul has no thought or passion, but the body is concerned in it; the body has no action or motion, but what in some degree effects the soul" (*SC* 214). Gestures, bodies in movement and rest, thoughts put into words, ideas expressed in song, symbols for eyes and ears — all these outward acts "are necessary to support inward tempers." God has made us so, and a flourishing prayer will not deny it.

Habits take time to establish. None of Law's advice suggests that there is a quick way to bring our hearts within the frame of God's will. We are merely foolish when we imagine we can wake up one morning and determine "From now on, I shall live a good life." This is why most New Year's resolutions are childish, wide-eyed, and helpless as fawns. Law is encouragingly frank here. The unhappy truth, as he sees it, is that we do not seriously intend to live as the gospel commands:

If you will here stop, and ask yourselves, why you are not as pious as the primitive Christians were, your own heart will tell you, that it is...purely because you never thoroughly intended it. (*SC* 57)

Intention, though, must be precise, even modest, or it will evaporate in the vast vagueness of its object. Law suggests that sin mostly takes the undramatic form of what an earlier age called "sloth." We do not so much will evil as suffer flabbiness in willing anything; we just go along with our desires as they spread over many things. Without a rule by which to realize themselves, Law insists, our intentions remain broken-backed. Intentions, then, must be precise in their object and executed methodically.

> If a man, whenever he was in company, where any one... spoke evil of his neighbour, should make it a rule to himself, either gently to reprove him, or...to leave the company as decently as he could,...this little rule, like a little leaven hid in a great quantity of meal, would spread and extend itself through the whole form of his life. (*SC* 112)

We begin piecemeal and so find "how little and small matters are the first steps and natural beginnings of great perfection" (*SC* 112).

This certainly is helpful advice, even though we might find Law a little too optimistic in his eighteenth-century faith in method. Underlying Law's realism, though, about the time that it takes for us to form worthy habits, there is a hugely important theological implication. Law has already told us that we are pressed for time, that now is the moment to take up our cross and follow the One who "comes quickly." He has made it quite clear, too, that God demands all, that he demands perfection. We owe God nothing less than everything, and we owe it now. The command for perfection is already upon us, and we are already behind-hand. Yet, without any slackening of this seriousness and this urgency, Law now tells us that we must and will take time, that the movement of heart and will is enough, indeed, is everything.

It is as if, within the relentless demand of God that never slackens, a space has opened up, a place of peace, in which the slow forming of the heart may take place. Perhaps this is why Law was so surprised by Wesley's criticism: that from Law's point of view, the advice that he gives in *A Serious Call* would make no sense without this space of friendship that God has established and within which change has time. This space, of course, is ours in Christ, and our entry into it in faith is "justification." We are thus made right with God, though not yet righteous in ourselves, not yet holy. Without this justification, without this gift of love given to those "yet sinners," fear and despair would be the proper response to Law's urgent and consuming God. That, however, is not the case. Neither fear nor great achievements make our true holiness on earth. Instead, the distinguishing mark of the saint, Law argues, is gratitude: "The greatest saint in the world . . . is he who is always thankful to God, who wills everything that God willeth, who receives everything as an instance of God's goodness, and has a heart always ready to praise God for it" (*SC* 218).

Humility after Breakfast

We now look a little closer at two sections of the devout and holy day: the prayers for 9:00 a.m. and for midday. By 9:00 a.m., the early rising Christian will be ready to observe another period of prayer and reflection. Law is too wise to tell us how long we are to spend in devotion; that must be dictated by personal circumstances. Only so may the way of holiness be a way for all. Perhaps Law might say: long enough to be serious, short enough to permit all our other God-given duties. Our prayers and meditations at 9:00 a.m. are to circle around the theme of "humility" — not, of course, as a merely intellectual exercise, but as a strategy of formation. We are to stoke our desire for humility, sharpen our understanding of it, determine our will for it, and appeal to God to lead us in the way of humility. This is not just another virtue, as far as Law is concerned. Humility is the virtue of virtues; it is the condition without which all virtues are compromised. As we will see, true love, the love of Jesus, and, therefore, the love demanded of us, is necessarily humble. So important is humility that Law claims that "we may as well think to see without eyes, or live without breath, as to live in the spirit of religion without the spirit of humility" (*SC* 228). When we look a little more closely, we understand that humility is the mirror for seeing Jesus; it is central because it is distinctive of him. Humility lies at the root of Christ's saving work as the one "who, being in the form of God . . . made himself of no reputation, and took upon him the form of a servant" (Phil. 2:6–7). Humility is what divides Christ from the world; it is the fulcrum of their necessary opposition. Thus, the humble person joins Christ in rejecting and being rejected by the world: "The servant is not greater than his lord. If they have persecuted me, they will also persecute you" (John 15:20). We will return to this later, but understanding the place that Law gives to humility requires that we, instead of thinking about humility abstractly, consider it in the closest relation to the story of Jesus.

Christians need to watch their language. Not always in the conventional sense — most sermons would gain in zest and immediacy for a judicious vulgarity or two. Christians need to watch their language because it gets confused in the rough and tumble of history and gets reduced, for the convenience of the old Adam, into smooth and insubstantial vagaries. With all the cultural and historical forces that, not without our help, serve to distort, twist, and muddle the terms, images, metaphors, and stories of Christian discourse, Christians will always need to do ambulance work on words.[3] History has made no little wreckage of "humility." Law himself admits that it is "the least understood, the least regarded, the least intended, the least desired and sought after, of all other virtues" (*SC* 228). The situation today is, if anything, worse. We have some place for humility, of course, generally commending it in those who bear their gifts or wealth lightly. For the most part, though, preaching humility is swimming against the cultural torrent; we do not even accord it the same degree of notional regard as did earlier, less democratically conscious times. Law would warn us, though, against a simply cultural explanation. If we resist humility, it is because it is a dangerous virtue, a peculiarly Christlike virtue and, therefore, just asking for crucifixion.

Unfortunately, "humility" has been damned by association, and since the publication of Dickens's *David Copperfield*, we remember it in the ghastly company of Uriah Heep, whose "damp fishy fingers" and oily insistence on his "umbleness" warn of calculating malice. Heep entered our culture with such force that he has haunted our ideas of humility for generations, even though only relatively few have ever met him in print.[4]

> "Be umble, Uriah," says father to me, "and you'll get on. It was what was always being dinned into you and me at school; it's what goes down best...." "When I was quite a young boy," said Uriah, "I got to know what umbleness did, and I took to it. I ate umble pie with an appetite....I am very umble to the present moment, Master Copperfield, but I've got a little power!"[5]

Uriah has given humility a bad name. Nevertheless, he points, despite himself, to the heart of humility, as Law understands it. Heep's sniveling references to his lowly station irritate but are not what makes him evil; rather, his evil lies in his being, above all, a liar. The bowing and scraping, the little services, and the self-negation are the tools of manipulation. Uriah uses his apparent weakness, his nonentity, as the means of exploitation; he works the hooks until he has "got a little power!" This "umbleness" is the demonic inversion of the humility that Law finds in the Gospels, where humility is the performance of truth.

Humility is the achievement of honesty before God, before ourselves, and before our neighbors. The humble person simply embraces as much reality as a human being can take. Humility is founded in a "true and just" sense of our condition, not on sporting "a worse opinion of ourselves than we deserve" (*SC* 229). In relation to God, that means recognizing how complete is our dependence on God, how we do not merely receive gifts from God but rather *are* the gift of God, one of innumerable forms of God's generosity. We are honest to God and true to ourselves not when we are proud, even of laudable achievements, but rather when we are grateful. Our lives do not bear much examining, Law reminds us; they are, for one thing, too ridiculous. Immediate desires dictate to our reason, and our reason seldom fails to come up with a good excuse for them. Our sense of dignity is based on the edited life that we show the world and preserve because God has not granted us telepathy. Not that Christians should make public sport of their errors and misjudgments, embarrassing thoughts and fantasies. Truthfulness, though, demands that we do not believe our own propaganda, so, to the extent that we are humble, we cannot regard ourselves without a wry smile. Our dignity lies not in ourselves but rather in Christ, in being those for whom he died. Finally, and tragically, we are more than foolish: we are enemies to life. Our sin has made us "abominable and odious to Him that made us" (*SC* 232). Consequently, our neighbors suffer from us: we regard them so little, only through the squint of our own interests. If we are humble, we take a larger view; we see them as the image of God, and we "strive to love the world, as God loves it" (*SC* 257). Men and women are infinitely beloved, greatly gifted, desperately vulnerable, and deadly in their destructiveness. Humility is life within the coordinates of these truths.

In the life of the Christian, then, truth must take the form of humility. By living a humble life, as Law has explained it, the Christian tells the truth about humanity. In the work of love, Christians make their argument against the world and for the freedom of Christ. We make that "practical" case through our gratitude to God, through clear-sightedness about ourselves, through forgiveness, by taking responsibility without arrogance, and by relieving our neighbors from the burden of our pride. The freedom that we represent here is specifically the freedom of Christ. Only as those conformed to the crucified Jesus, who are dead to the world, are Christians free "in a world where glory itself is false" (*SC* 260). Law goes on to expound this vital link between humility and freedom in two chapters devoted to the education of males and females.

Eighteenth-century clergy, social reformers, and intelligentsia placed great faith in education. The philosopher John Locke set the tone of enlightened educational hope: "Of all the Men we meet with, Nine parts of Ten are what they are, Good or Evil, useful or not, by their Education. 'Tis that which makes the great difference in Mankind."[6] Law is not unusual, then, in stressing the significance of education, and some of the practices that he deplores came in for fairly routine clerical disapproval. He is distinctively forceful, of course, and his rigorism savages behavior at which others might wink. He is interestingly bold, too, particularly in his treatment of women. Female education comes in for especially severe judgment partly because Law recognizes the vital influence of mothers in early childhood, nicely remarking that "as we call our first language our mother-tongue, so we may as justly call our first tempers our mother-tempers"(*SC* 261). More than that, though, Law regards the conventional genteel education given to young women as an even greater travesty upon human dignity than that of young men. Women are brought up to a subservient foolishness, a vain existence for male amusement, that disguises their potential for intellectual achievement and spiritual wisdom. Notable though this is, what distinguishes the educational chapters in *A Serious Call* is not any apparently progressive notions but rather Law's rigorous insistence on the total revolution of mind, heart, and practice required by Christianity: "Humility ... cannot subsist in any mind, but so far as it is dead to the world" (*SC* 238). Again, it is Christ who establishes the distinction. There is the education of the world and the education of the cross, and no compromise is possible between them. Law is not proposing that in all and every respect the *content* of a Christian education should be different from a "worldly" one; rather, he is pointing to a fundamental character: what ultimately should an education dispose us toward? Law proposes that the world educates for pride, to glorify the self or the group. The driving energy is competition. By contrast, a Christian education should form us in those truths that constitute humility, that glorify God. The energy that moves here is the love that loves as God does.

"Dead to the world," crucified with Christ, the Christian is free from the world's judgment, as well as God's. "Many a man would often drop a resentment, and forgive an affront, but that he is afraid if he should, the world would not forgive him" (*SC* 238). Confidence in our individuality, in having our own opinions, is self-deceit; generally, we are merely the dolls of that ventriloquist "culture." From a very early age, Law thunders, we are taught to value what is beneath those who bear the image of God:

> According to the spirit and vogue of this world, whose corrupt air we have all breathed, there are many things that pass for great and honourable, and most desirable, which yet are so far from being so, that the true greatness and honour of our nature consists in the not desiring them. (*SC* 237)

Education is a training in competitiveness; we learn to think less of ourselves when others flourish, and more when others fail. Like little sponges, we soak up the enthusiasms around us, "absorb the torrent of worldly fashions and opinions" (*SC* 237). Thus, we become perilously vulnerable. I live in a city of students in a culture that celebrates youthfulness. As I pass the age of fifty, I look more and more like someone's father, which, in fact, I am. The young clerk at the checkout appears to be wondering why I am still here. Are there not homes for people like me? Should I not be dead or something? I find this hard, not just because running now makes me wheeze and fret, but also because I have bought a lie about aging. Education, in school and out of it, from its beginnings in parental cooing through our adulthood immersion in society, sets us to "live and die slaves to the customs and temper of the world" (SC 237). This grim verdict invites the reasonable protest that it is just too extreme, that it lumps together much that is good with all that is bad. Law, though, shows no interest in denying that some educational practices are relatively better than others. His critique expresses the *theological* judgment that begins when Jesus finds himself a stranger in the world and reaches its climax when he is crucified. Everything human is bracketed within this judgment, just as in the Gospel narratives the same judgment embraces the fleeing disciples and the fickle crowd, Romans and Jews, righteous and "sinners." "Pride" is not just the haughty superiority of a certain class; it names the root desire to be our own happiness. That desire informs all our ways and so expresses itself also in the judgments that education and society train us to make: "How many people swell with pride and vanity, for such things as they would not know how to value at all, but that they are admired in the world" (SC 237).

We are creatures of education, and an education that reproduces the lineaments of pride in us all. Nevertheless, though its influence penetrates and spreads throughout our lives, "it is all built upon a blind obedience; and we need only open our eyes to get quit of its power" (SC 238). Our obedience is "blind" because it is not based on truth. The "world" of the sinner, the world that Jesus has overcome, is not reality but rather its unhappy likeness — the construction, in language, practices, and things, of a dwelling apart from life's Source. To use one of Law's favorite metaphors, it is a dream of seeing. Humility, on the other hand, is wide awake. The humble person is free from the world, free from its judgment, free from its threatening conformity, because she takes her bearings from the cross. The crucified Christ is the measure of our ruin: "How monstrous and shameful the nature of sin is, is sufficiently apparent from that great Atonement, that is necessary to cleanse us from the guilt of it" (*SC* 231). The cross, though, is also that "great conquest over the world" from which Christians receive their freedom and vocation. We are humble insofar as we are conformed to the self-humbling of the Son of God. He has freed us from the pride with which the world trades, its demands and strictures and expectations. We are ready for the boldness of godly love: for listening to hard truths about ourselves, for honesty when lies are in our interest, for charity to those judged undeserving, for peacemaking when violence is defended. The freedom that is humility also liberates others. Law gives us an important example. From one culture to another, people who are poor identify shame and humiliation as one of poverty's harshest burdens. This humiliation derives from the way poverty makes outsiders of the poor. Humility, however, which sees others as divinely loved and ourselves as needing no less mercy than anyone else, "will keep you from all vain and proud thoughts of your own state and distinction in life, and from treating the poor as creatures of a different species" (*SC* 274).

A humble life, of course, is not the creation of a day, which is why Law places it within each day's devotion. This steadying, careful attention to reality runs counter not only to "the world" but also to ourselves, to our will that is not yet tuned to Christ and to our own formation in the world's ways. There is a world of unlearning to do. With respect to humility, the Christian "is to forget and lay aside his own spirit, which has been a long while fixing and forming itself" (*SC* 236).

Humility is gradually attained, Law suggests, by holding before ourselves the goodness of God and meditating on the lives of Jesus and the apostles; by attempting as much honesty with ourselves as we can stand; and by acts of love through simple daily practices that put first the good of others. "Let every day, therefore, be a day of humility; condescend to all the weaknesses and infirmities of your fellow-creatures,... be a servant of servants, and condescend to do the lowest offices to the lowest of mankind" (*SC* 259). This, of course, recalls the One who came "not to be served but to serve." What appears in the working of humility, gradually and not without many reversals, is nothing short of the form of Christ, his Spirit in our flesh.

Love before Lunch

For the biblical "sixth hour," or twelve noon, Law chose the theme of "universal love," by which he intends that love to which all Christians are called as disciples of Christ and children of God. To this theme, and as its expression during the time of devotion, he attaches the practice of intercessory prayer. The link is clear. Intercessory prayer is a primary act of Christian love. As such, it has a formative and guiding role with respect to all our other acts of love. Across the day, Law's choice of times and themes has its particular logic. There is an obvious progression. The day begins with praise and thanksgiving, gratitude and delight being the original form of our relationship with God and the substance of our eternal return. Humility follows as the form of our lives in the world and as the likeness of Christ that flourishes in love and prayer. The twin theme of love and intercession is properly placed before that for 3:00 p.m., "the nature and duty of conformity to the will of God, in all our actions and designs" (*SC* 316). Intercession precedes such conformity or "resignation" because God is not "fate" but rather love, because our intercession is not beating the air but rather is made to One who hears us. God, though, is also free, with an understanding of our good beyond our most visionary moments. He is not bound by our wishes, and only idols can be manipulated. So, having prayed, we hand ourselves over to God's answer, accepting and obeying God's will with a thankful, humble heart, having already turned to our Father in prayer. Confession finishes the day and is Law's final theme. He closes the devout and holy day with this because it is good to keep short accounts and because, before we sleep, we should reflect upon the day. Sleep, though, is the simulacrum of death. Each day, therefore, becomes an anticipation and metaphor of a "good death." We reflect and confess our sins and failings, not sourly or morbidly, of course, but rather with frank and simple confidence in the God who has done everything needful for our forgiveness.

The discussion of intercession is preceded by an exposition of Christian love. Law begins with a crucial point. In John's Gospel, Jesus describes the commandment to love as a "new commandment," but what about it is new? "Love one another," in and of itself, is not new, "for this was an old precept, both of the law of Moses, and of nature" (*SC* 288). The novelty consists not in loving but rather in loving "as Christ has loved us." This love is "universal," without respect of persons. As with humility, the meaning of Christian love and, therefore, of intercession is given in Christ. Law seems to blur his christological focus, though, with his list of five reasons why Christian love must be "universal." First, he writes, this is a matter of justice. We seek our own good, and we do so wholeheartedly, if not always with happy results. It is unjust not to extend such love to those who are, after all, "so exactly of the same nature, and in the same condition as ourselves" (*SC* 296). Then, second, this love is commanded by God, and, third, it is our obligation as the children of God, called to imitate our heavenly Father, "who willeth the happiness of all His creatures, and maketh His sun to rise on the evil, and on the good" (*SC* 296). Only now do we come to two appeals to Christ: the second is simply that Christ commands us to love, and the first that "our redemption by Jesus Christ calleth us to the exercise of this love, who came from Heaven and laid down His life, out of love to the whole sinful world" (*SC* 296). Law concludes with a flourish: "These are the great, perpetual reasons, on which our obligation to love all mankind as ourselves is founded" (*SC* 296). The list, though, is rather a hodge-podge for such "great and perpetual reasons." They are not all of the same kind or, surely, of the same weight.

Unlike "God commands it," perhaps, Law's opening reason is not freestanding but rather depends on arguments given elsewhere. On its own, one might retort that the justice of self-love actually limits our obligations to others, especially in conditions where desired goods are scarce. The two appeals to divine commandment are important, but they beg the question of how the two commands are related, especially as they are significantly different: God commands us to "love every man as ourself," while Christ commands us "to love one another as he has loved us." Earlier, Law argued that the former was "an old precept, both of the law of Moses, and of nature" (*SC* 288), so the two must be different in content. So how? And in what way are they related? Law's third and fourth reasons have more specific content. Again, one appeals to God, the other to Jesus. The first grounds the love command in God's universal goodness as Creator. This is an account of love that, like the command "love every man as oneself," carries no immediate reference to God's work of salvation. As a response to Christ, however, the obligation to love refers specifically to the atonement. So, whereas the appeal to God's care as Creator gives us a love that is just and impartial, maintaining the divine order for the good and bad without respect of persons, the appeal to Christ faces us with a love directed specifically at enemies. This is the radical love of the gospel and of the One who died for us "while we were yet sinners" (Rom. 5:8). This is the "new commandment" based on Jesus' "new example of love." Christ's love fulfills the care that God shows for creation and exceeds it as the reconciliation of enemies. Only in Christ do we recognize the depths and heights of divine love. This is in keeping with the Christ-centered interpretation that

Law gives of humility: "The state of Christianity implieth nothing else, but an entire, absolute conformity to that spirit which Christ showed in the mysterious Sacrifice of Himself upon the Cross" (SC 241). Far more than may appear on the surface, the person and work of Christ are at the center of Law's thought. Since an account of Christ as Savior will be vital to any discussion of "grace and works," it may be that Wesley and others, who found Law so graceless, were not reading closely enough to recognize the christological pulse of his arguments. In fairness to those critics, though, we must admit that Law did not always make it easy.

Christian love is "universal"; it has no favorites, and there is no one beyond the pale. Universal in extent, it is also universal in depth; there is no good, however trivial, beneath the dignity of Christian love, no human need beyond our concern. How is this universality redefined, though, when we "love as Christ loved us"? As we have seen, in Christ, God loves enemies. This love is reconciling and peacemaking. Such terms are so well worn, so dangerously "nice," that we may miss the reach of this love. "How monstrous," Law writes, "and how shameful the nature of sin is, is sufficiently apparent from that great Atonement, that is necessary to cleanse us from the guilt of it" (SC 231). God embraces godlessness, finds the way into a world that does all in its power to exclude him. He suffers its denial and scorn, and then he makes the very climax of its hatred the means of forgiveness. Not only faithful to the created order, maintaining it as a source of life for good and bad alike, God seeks out the lost, turns toward his enemies, runs after those who flee from him. This is the measure of "universal" love. However, whereas sin is a common condition, forgiveness is particular. God's reconciliation addresses the disease that cripples and deforms each one of us. We are not redeemed alone but neither are we redeemed in the gross. Christ lifts the burden that is everyone's yet all our own, leading each one of us back through the tangled paths that we ourselves chose when we went the way Adam sent us.

> You are as much the care of this great God and Father of all worlds and all spirits, as if He had no son but you, or there was no creature for Him to love and protect but you alone.
>
> (SC 255)

God's love is particular and finds its completion in the singularity of our healing. The upshot of all this is that Christian love is universal but not general. Though its object is truly "all sorts and conditions" of humanity, this love is not dissipated in general goodwill but rather is realized in specific service. Since, too, we are to love as "Christ loved us," the final test of Christian love is the way we deal with enemies and with sin as we meet it in our neighbors. "No one is of the Spirit of Christ, but he that has the utmost compassion for sinners. Nor is there any greater sign of your own perfection, than when you find yourself all love and compassion towards them that are very weak and defective" (SC 294). And when the sinner is also our enemy, there is still no escape, for Christian perfection binds us to the tough work of forgiveness.

Christians, then, obey the command to love not as "a command of Moses and nature" but rather as following Christ's "new example of love." We observe (at the risk of anticipating the next chapter) that Christians confess Jesus as the perfect coincidence of God's love and the obedience and self-giving of a human being. In Christ, God takes our humanity and makes it the unsurpassable expression of his love. If, as Law says, Christianity is no more or less than life formed in the Spirit of Christ, then the "new commandment" takes us into the universal love of God, not only to follow a benevolence commanded by Moses and indicated by nature but also to put into flesh God's unbounded, reconciling love. We do this, too, not because we have discovered a "higher way of loving" but rather because God has made our humanity his own and thus raised it. Grace precedes. The possibility of fulfilling this commandment is not ours but rather is given to us in Christ, who went before us whither, until then, we would not and could not go.

Law gathers up his teaching on intercession in the character sketch of the parish priest, Ouranius (Heavenly). Ouranius did not secure the clerical career that his ambition had mapped out for him. Instead, he ended up in a parish notable only for remoteness from anyone whom Ouranius considered civilized company. He kept, therefore, to his study, substituting books for flesh and blood, possibly reassuring himself that the authors, though dead, at least were decent. He lived one caricature of the eighteenth-century Anglican cleric:

> He kept much at home, writ notes upon Homer and Plautus, and sometimes thought it hard to be called to pray by any poor body, when he was just in the midst of one of Homer's battles. (SC 304)

The "poor body," though, may have wished that Ouranius had stayed in Troy or received the point of a spear more real than imaginary. "He had a haughtiness in his temper, a great contempt and disregard for all foolish and unreasonable people" (SC 303) — anyone, we suppose, unlike himself. Yet Ouranius changed. Once disdainful of those in his charge, "he can now not only converse with, but gladly attend and wait upon the poorest kind of people . . . in the spirit of his Lord and Master girds himself, and is glad to kneel down and wash any of their feet" (SC 304).

This inward revolution was the fruit of prayer. Ouranius began to pray for his parishioners, and the practice of prayer shaped the heart that prayed into the intercessor that prayer and people needed. Intercession "softens his heart, enlightens his mind, sweetens his temper," and demands that he bring his parishioners more sharply before his mind (SC 303). Perhaps all this began with going through the motions, with mouthing concern, but prayer has now become concern, indeed ambition for those whose names and lives he lifts to God. Their cares, pleasures, questions, failings, and sins no longer are repellent; they are life and death. He "never thinks he can esteem, reverence, or serve those enough, for whom he implores so many mercies from God" (*SC* 305). Ouranius no longer judges his poor neighbors according to the pecking order of class, education, and wealth. How could he? They have burst such confines and become those to whom God wishes joy, for whom Christ died. Prayer has lifted Ouranius into the discourse of God's desire.

Is Law suggesting that we pray to benefit ourselves, in order to improve our tempers, polish up our inner lives, become better-quality people? This would be an easy mistake to make, turning prayer into self-cultivation, especially as Law does point to definite improvements in Ouranius's character. Are such "strategies of formation" really the devices of self-concern disguised by religion? Law's teaching on intercession, though, reminds us that all such "strategies" involve handing ourselves over to the work of God. Ouranius is not cultivating his inner life, for that would merely be the pious equivalent of sitting in his study reading Homer. Intercession has turned this man inside out. Though Ouranius is doing the praying, he is not cultivating himself; rather, he is being formed from beyond himself, for the sake of neighbors who are not means to his ends, by a God who desires for us far more than we know.

When we pray for others, we meet again the demand, essential to Christian love, for both the universal and the particular. We must allow our prayers to roam the distance, flying toward the far reaches of God's concern, interceding for men and women in places and conditions of which we have the barest inkling. Prayer, though, must also settle somewhere; it must nest in particular places. We will pray for those within our view, whose daily lives and yearly changes we see and toward whom we may extend other deeds of love. Intercession brings people into a clearer focus and demands that we inform ourselves. We should not settle for vagueness, when detailed knowledge is possible. Prayer thus enlarges our capacity for others, trains us in specificity, and weans us away from self-protective generalizations and the safety of not finding out. Prayer demands attentiveness in order to provide the material for intercession, a willingness to watch and listen. Of course, the practice of interceding demands the offering of our actions as instruments of God's answer. As Law notes, if Ouranius's

> whole life is one continual exercise of great zeal and labour, hardly ever satisfied with any degrees of care and watchfulness, it is because he has learned the great value of souls, by so often appearing before God as an intercessor for them.
>
> (*SC* 303)

On the other hand, if one more actively minded is tempted to suggest cutting out the prayer and heading straight for "practical" service, Law would warn that this is the path to harm. Here we see why it is so important to understand intercession as a strategy of formation. Prayer is not just something we do; still less is it merely a ritual of working through lists of our own devising. Rather, when we apply ourselves to intercession, we lose a degree of the hold that we have on ourselves. Prayer begins to form us, grasping "the government of our heart," leading us into God before we inflict ourselves on the general or particular populace. Intercession is the act of love prior to the acts of love. In lively prayer for others, intercession ceases to be "our" business. God, thankfully, comes to stand between us and our neighbors, shaping and guiding us in the difficult business of love.

Ouranius, of course, is one of Law's idealized characters. He has had his crisis and now achieved the rhythms of a holy life. This simple "before and after" structure makes the general point with nice economy but at the price of underplaying the persistent ambiguities of a Christian life. In truth, the movement from coldness to commitment continues throughout our days. Law certainly bears serious witness to the warming of the heart that arises in the practice of devotion, sweetening the temper and enlivening the mind. He does not, however, consider intercession as dependent upon or driven by the way we feel about those for whom we pray. The will to pray precedes emotions of love or compassion, and it will always exceed such emotions. The heart's delight is not the precondition of prayer. Prayer begins in doing what we are told, in willing to pray, trying to pray, persisting in prayer. Law is confident that prayer will come to form us, to take over the process, sometimes more so, sometimes less. However, we will never be rid of his advice to take the "proper means," to prepare for God through the *practice* of devotion. No act of love will need this wisdom more than that which especially bears Christ's signature: prayer and love for enemies. Here, much of the time, we must bear the burden of our own anger and fear, and keep on praying even though the words are like ashes. So, despite our feelings, we are conformed to Christ's sacrifice.

A Serious Call to the Gospel?

> Be as happy as the world can make thee, all is but sleeping and dreaming, and what is still worse, it is like sleeping in a ship when thou should be pumping out the water. (*CP* 19)

Law's practical treatises are a wakeup call to those asleep in disaster. They are, perhaps, the finest spiritual alarm calls written in English. Both works eventually secured a very broad readership from all social classes, ironically, in some measure because of Wesley's recommendation and abridged versions. The readers that Law himself had in mind, though, as we have noted, were those who by virtue of wealth and position possessed social influence and leadership — the man of business in the town, but particularly, those who controlled the countryside, the farms, villages, and small towns. In what was still very much a rural country, the social power of the landowner, from the local squire to the grandee, determined the lives of most English men and women. Among these social classes, Law is addressing a spiritual disease, that of complacency. Too many sit on the laurels of churchgoing, respectability, birth in a "nation of Christians," and, of course, reasonableness. This complacency, Law recognized, had found some purchase in Christian teaching and theology. Are we not justified by "faith alone"? Did not Christ bear all burdens "in our place"? In opposition to this travesty of good news, Law throws the weight of his treatises on the gospel's fierce demand for change. He will leave evasion without excuse. Christ did not

go the way of obedience to relieve us of the trouble of discipleship. He did not die "in our place" as one who takes from us the
eager demands of God. He died, Law stresses, as our "representative," going before us and making it possible for us to follow.
Law's polemic is against what Dietrich Bonhoeffer, centuries later,
described as "cheap grace."

> Cheap grace means the justification of sin without the jus-
> tification of the sinner. Grace alone does everything, they
> say, and so everything can remain as it was before.... Cheap
> grace is the preaching of forgiveness without requiring
> repentance, baptism without church discipline, Commu-
> nion without confessions. Cheap grace is grace without
> discipleship.[1]

Is it enough, then, to say that Wesley and the evangelicals missed
the point? This teaching was for the complacent, not for folk of
such terrific earnestness as they. Law was not writing the book
on grace; he assumes grace and expounds God's demand, the discipleship that distinguishes the reality of God's salvation from
cheap grace. His own encapsulation of Christianity, ventured in
conversation with Wesley, was a simple statement of the priority
of grace: "Religion is the most plain, simple thing in the world; it
is only, 'We love Him because He first loved us.' "[2] God's loving
act is prior, though Law is careful to choose a summary that in-
cludes our response, awoken by God's love. There is no reason to
think that Law ever forgot, let alone abandoned, this conviction
while he wrote *Christian Perfection* and *A Serious Call*. He can
hardly be blamed for failing to answer questions that he was not,
at that point, posing.

Still, though, the riposte may be too easy. The significance of
our labors before God, what it means to "work out your own
salvation in fear and trembling" (Phil. 2:12), depends upon how
we understand "the benefits of Christ" and the conditions upon
which we enjoy them. A book on Christian devotion in which

the horizon of grace was absent or obscured would indeed need "gospelizing," the treatment that Whitefield suggested for *A Serious Call*. We have seen the signs that Law founds the holy life on God's love: the confident tone that persists through all the warnings; the respect that Law has for gradual progress and simple but firmly intended steps to holiness; his lack of legalism; his flexibility; and the constant stress upon intention rather than performance. Law is strikingly cautious, too, when it comes to the consequences of ignoring the summons to Christian integrity. He is very wary of foreclosing the reach of God's mercy. Even in connection with the wretchedly frivolous and hypocritical Flavia, he notes, "I shall not take upon me to say, that it is impossible for Flavia to be saved; but...she has no grounds from Scripture to think she is in the way of salvation" (*SC* 108).

Beyond these general indicators, though, is there any point at which we can see more clearly how Law conceived the relationship between God's action and our own, or, to put it more concretely: since Jesus does not take away our responsibility, how it is that he helps us?

I have stressed the extent to which Jesus Christ, sometimes despite appearances, is the determining core of Law's account of holiness. Law also formulates this explicitly: "The Christian's great conquest over the world is all contained in the mystery of Christ upon the Cross" (*SC* 241). Here is the point from which to unravel the relationship between the primacy of God's love and the possibility of our faithfulness. Law's initial expansion of "the mystery of Christ upon the Cross," though, is not particularly encouraging. "It was there, and from thence, that He taught all Christians how they were to come out of, and conquer the world, and what they were to do in order to be His disciples" (*SC* 241). This suggests that Jesus' sacrifice is merely exemplary — a position characteristic of Deists, such as Matthew Tindal, who rejected any account of salvation that did not consist in a human moral initiative, to be rewarded with God's approval. Law, however, understands Jesus as achieving for us something that we cannot achieve for ourselves. His love, which is the love of God incarnate, is the divine love that goes before ours and makes our human discipleship possible. Jesus suffered as "our Representative . . . with such particular merit, as to make our joining with Him acceptable unto God. He suffered, and was a Sacrifice, to make our sufferings and sacrifice of ourselves fit to be received by God" (*SC* 242). We should be unwise to take this as Law's full statement on the atonement, but it does suggest how he coordinates our efforts with Christ's work. Law nowhere compromises on the darkness of sin, that "deplorable corruption." Our best works are deeply ambiguous, our finest motives still impure. We are not in a position to glory before God in our own righteousness. We fall short. "They are all gone out of the way, they are together become unprofitable; there is none that doeth good, no, not one" (Rom. 3:12). Only the representative life and death of Jesus makes the ambiguous efforts of sinners acceptable to God. The "Son of God" suffered that "He might render God propitious to that nature in which He suffered" (*SC* 336). Only on the basis of Christ, and through our union with him in faith, are the ungodly justified. Justification, though, makes works possible; it does not free us from them. That would be "cheap grace." More precisely, it would mean that Christ's work voided our calling rather than reestablishing it, making it possible. Thus, in a work written toward the end of his life, Law would affirm, following the Epistle of James, that "works prove faith to be living; want of works prove faith to be dead."[3] Law does not regard faith as "inadequate" but rather teaches that a living faith in Christ issues in works as its natural expression. Why? Because salvation is more than forgiveness; it is renewal and restoration, being brought once more into our inheritance and vocation as the people of God.

All this may be put with a slightly different emphasis. The human vocation has not gone unfulfilled. "Humanity" is not the name for creatures condemned to live always as unkept promises. Jesus has fulfilled our vocation and realized the promise given with human nature: "You are my son, my beloved." Christ has obeyed God's serious call upon human life, that all-encompassing call outside which human life is estranged from itself. Christ does this as the incarnate Word, the Son of God. It is God who answers "the serious call to a devout and holy life" by uniting himself with humanity so that humanity partakes of God. This is the acceptable life, the way of return from "world" to reality. If we have the Spirit of Christ — and there is no Christian faith without it — we will be conformed to Christ's sufferings, his way of departure from the world. We enter the "mystery of Christ upon the Cross" as we recognize here God's love for us and as we are so united with Christ that, through His Spirit, we embrace, in our turn, the "serious call." "Justification," in Law's view, never meant only that God declares us righteous but always that he also makes us righteous.

In expounding Law's teaching, have I read a good deal more into *A Serious Call* than is even implicitly there? Have I constructed a doctrine of grace *for* Law rather than *from* his writing? That later work on justification, though, which takes the form of a dialogue between a Methodist and a "Churchman," is quite clear that all good works are works of divine grace:

> What true Christian ever called good works our own works? Does not scripture say, "it is God who worketh in us, both to will, and to do"? Now if your faith may be called good and saving, because it is God's gift, and power within you; then a Christian's works may be called good and saving . . . because they are all wrought in God, and by his power working in him.[4]

The explicit references to grace are relatively few in *A Serious Call*. That alone gives some purchase to Law's evangelical critics. Read carefully, though, the references are telling and in keeping with the fuller statement above. Christians "partake of the Divine nature," grace is the environment in which their own efforts take place. God's assisting grace — his active, enlivening love — is always present, hidden but intimate, and it should be called upon at all times. True devotion is always the gift of God, never a human work:

> From this, it goes without saying that grace is needful: for though the spirit of devotion is the gift of God, and not attainable by any mere power of our own, yet it is mostly given to, and never withheld from, those who, by a wise and diligent use of proper means, prepare themselves for the reception of it. (*SC* 203)

This is a careful statement. Indeed, grace is "mostly" given to those who prepare for it. Yet, Law does not limit God's grace. God may call the unprepared, convict the heedless sinner in the midst of his cups, convert the persecutor. Still, we may have confidence that if we ask, we will receive. And if God's grants, he does so, of course, in grace. *Christian Perfection* and *A Serious Call* are about lives lived in the environment of grace. They treat of Christian discipleship as seen from the perspective of our responsibility. In advocating strategies of formation, Law teaches us not how to live without grace but rather how to receive it and how to make our days a constant cry for the mercy without which we cannot live. Despite Wesley's critique, as this superb prayer shows, Law expected nothing except as the gift of Christ:

> O Holy Jesus, Son of the most High God, Thou that wast scourged at a pillar, stretched and nailed upon a cross, for the sins of the world, unite me to Thy cross, and fill my soul with Thy holy, humble, and suffering spirit.... Thou that didst cleanse the lepers, heal the sick, and give sight to the blind, cleanse my heart, heal the disorders of my soul, and fill me with heavenly light. (*SC* 199–200)

Chapter 6 ———————————————————

The Great and Mysterious Story

From Narrow to Wide Focus

Law's literary career divides rather conveniently. There are the practical treatises and various polemical works of the 1720s and 1730s, and then, beginning with *The Grounds and Reasons of Christian Regeneration* in 1739, we have the writings influenced by Jacob Boehme. Contemporaries recognized this convenient division equally clearly. The practical treatises were regarded as his masterpieces, whereas the "Behemist" works met with suspicion, sometimes fury. His readers liked being told that "the incomprehensible Trinity" is "eternally breaking forth" in "Eternal Nature" even less than they liked instructions to get up early and stop swearing. We can make too much of the contrast, though. Law never retracts his description of Christian perfection, and he would not have smiled on any suggestion that Boehme had taught him a milder, less rigorous road. The Behemist writings differ in style, introduce new concepts, and take more controversial doctrinal positions on the wrath of God, hell, and salvation. A deep connection, however, remains with the earlier works. In the practical treatises Law offered us a sharp, close-up account of Christian life; in the later works this is not abandoned, but the focus widens dramatically to take in the overarching story of creation, fall, and redemption, within which the Christian life makes the sense that it does.

Though Law took much from Boehme, he was no slavish follower. There is great difference of detail between them. Law simply ignored most of the teachings that are central to his hero. There is, too, a vast difference in climate.

Law always remained a teacher of Christian holiness. Boehme, however, in addition to guiding men and women into "the way of Christ," was a theosophist, a revealer of hidden wisdom concerning the Divine being. He recalls, for instance, a moment of ecstasy, an inbreaking to "the innermost Birth of the Deity" from where "my spirit suddenly saw through all, and in all created things, even in herbs and grass, I knew God . . . and suddenly in that Light my will was set upon by a mighty impulse to describe the being of God."[1] Law had no such impulse. He does not challenge the validity of Boehme's revelations. He ignores Boehme's daringly speculative teaching about God's own inner-divine birth from the *Ungrund*. The *Ungrund* is that Divine abyss in which God "brings Himself into a threefoldedness as to an apprehensibility of Himself."[2] Law sails past all this, keeping his theological craft close to what he thought strictly needful for Christian holiness. He urged his friend Thomas Langcake, "Put away all needless curiosity in Divine matters; and look upon everything to be so but that which helps you to die to yourself, that the spirit and life of Christ may be found in you."[3] What Law takes from Boehme he takes because he believes that it will help us to see more clearly why we must die to ourselves and live to Christ. He adopts elements of Boehme's retelling of creation and fall but resituates them in his own version. He derives his key concepts and images from Boehme, but he shapes, interprets, and reemphasizes them in a distinctive way. Law wants to show us that Christianity is the "heavenly Divine life offering itself again to the inward man, that had lost it" (*DK* 95). Under Boehme's influence, that Divine labor on our souls becomes the red thread of the entire story of creation, salvation, and consummation. In holiness we were created, and from the moment of our fall to the time at which all tears are dried, the work of Christ is our sanctification, the breaking out of God within us.

Law's intent, then, is practical, not speculative. We do not need our curiosity satisfied; we need only to be new born in Christ and formed by him. If this is so, why does Law spend so much time on what may well strike us as highly speculative? After all, Law dares, following Boehme, to fill in some of the Bible's deepest silences. He dwells on events hidden in shadows, such as "Nature" prior to time; the fall of angels and the ruin of their heavenly realm; the texture of life in Eden and Adam's paradisal condition; the creation of Eve; and the dynamics of our primal ancestors' tragedy. If Jesus and new birth in him is the heart of the matter, why all this rummaging around in matters almost beyond our imagination, let alone our understanding? The simple answer is that Law always stuck to the fundamental description of Christianity that he announced in *Christian Perfection*. Christianity encompasses "two great truths, the deplorable corruption of human nature, and its new birth in Christ Jesus." Only by attending closely to the fall and its consequences, Law claims, can we possibly understand our "deplorable condition," appreciate the necessity of our new birth, give right praise to the One who overcomes ruin and brings regeneration, and thus bow in joyful obedience to Jesus, who has received that "Name above all names." Though this new birth takes place in the few years of a human life, it is by no means dwarfed by the immensities of space and time; rather, its meaning can be measured only within the cosmic context sketched in these strange hints about the origins of Nature and history.

Myth Matters

Angelic fall, heaven divided, the innocence of paradise, original temptation — this is the stuff of what we generally refer to as "myth." "Myth," though, is a tricky term. Specialized meanings are found in anthropology, history, literary criticism, comparative religion, philosophy, and cultural studies; none of them are

uncontroversial, and all have their distinctive nuances.[4] Though
the word is quite modern, the variety of expositions, in theology alone are such that the question "What is myth?" is as likely
to provoke a history as a definition.[5] To make matters worse, in
popular usage "myth" is virtually equivalent to "nonsense," a dis-
missal of claims that are just plain false or, at best, fanciful yarns.
That Scottish men wear nothing beneath their kilts is a myth —
or, at least, I hope so. Despite the difficulties of definition though,
and the bewildering variety of the myths themselves, there are
a number of conclusions in recent discussion that will help us
understand William Law's rendering of biblical myth. First, myths
matter. However much scholars once fueled the word's more familiar use, today they are more likely to consider seriously the
"truth" that myths articulate. "Myth perhaps differs from story
in this, that questions of truth or falsehood are *inherently rele-
vant* to a myth in a way that they are not to a story."[6] What sort
of truth might we find here, though? The variety of myths pro-
hibits a single answer, but of biblical myth or myths such as *The
Epic of Gilgamesh*, Baldur's death, the love of Isis and Osiris, and
Prometheus, it is accurate to say that they "are marked by their
relevance to men's questions about their nature and place in the
universe."[7] They are not, as was once thought, primitive science,
and the truth of biblical myth is not that of reportage, despite
all the misguided Christian ink spent insisting otherwise. At no
time might one have peeked through leaves at a comely maiden
chatted up by a snake; no Eden hid an Eve who

> . . . half embracing leaned
> On our first Father, half her swelling breast
> Naked met his under the flowing gold
> Of her loose tresses hid.[8]

But that, of course, is not the point. Myths matter because, for
those whose myths they are, they present the inescapable conditions within which their lives take place: the powers that bear

down on them, the limits to their own, and the unmastered sources of sustenance and renewal. The myths thereby figure patterns of integrity for communities and their members; they prescribe duties, proscribe wrongdoing, and shape hopes.[9] Typically, mythological narratives are concerned with origins, with formative beginnings or changes to the possibilities from which life is lived. They treat of the "whence" and the "whither" of becoming. These origins, again, are not historically identifiable origins; the setting of myths is in a time before time, an age before the measurable years of common life but also a time always present or, as Paradise, present in its enduring absence. Myth addresses the future, too. As we will see, in Law's version of biblical myths the events take their full meaning from the futures that God opens up in creation and redemption. God answers angelic rebellion in the making of a new world, and human disobedience is met with promise and a living and persistent word implanted in the human heart. The mythical language used to tell of creation, the beginnings of suffering, the faring of our first parents, and the origins of evil gives an understanding of the world and the terms set for life and discloses a way of going about it. As such, we may certainly speak of truth and falsehood. Precisely that is at stake when the Hebrew author rejected the eternal cosmic matter in the Babylonian *Enuma Elish* in favor of the One Lord who creates everything by his word. Similarly, when the Romantic poet Shelley recast the Prometheus story in *Prometheus Unbound*, he did so in opposition to Christianity, to voice a different promise and different powers of life.

Myths, C. S. Lewis pointed out, are "extraliterary." Unlike a literary creation, such as a novel, they are not tied to a particular telling but rather are available for any number of renderings.[10] When they do receive literary form, as in Ovid's *Metamorphoses*, that form remains, however superb, one version, one interpretation, and not definitive. Dracula and Frankenstein have broken free of their literary creators for a cultural life of their own passing through many media: film, stage, painting, masks and costume, public holidays, games, and comic books. So much so that we remember their modern origins in Stoker and Shelley almost with surprise that anyone really *invented* them.[11] The history of a myth is the history of its retellings and reinterpretations. Law's is one such: a combinative telling of various biblical myths some of which are not explicitly in Scripture but rather are read into the Bible's hints and gaps. Law found in Boehme an apprehension of God's word in the form of remade myths. In his turn, he clarified, reshaped, and retold those myths as necessary to knowledge of "the deplorable corruption of human nature, and its new birth in Christ Jesus." In judging this reinterpretation, we must ask how well Law thus discerns the mystery of God in Jesus and how well he represents our lives in Christ. Finally, the mythical elements that Law takes from the Bible do not stand alone. They belong within the whole canon of Scripture as the mythical beginning of the story that comes down to Christ. The "tree of the knowledge of good and evil" and the time when "Quirinius was governor of Syria" do not exist on the same linear plane of time. The former speaks in myth the stern riddle answered in the latter. For the Christian, any myth-making, such as Law's, must be assessed, therefore, as to how it hangs together with Christ to retell the story of which he is the center, the One from whom and for whom all things are.

Did Law think that he was remaking biblical mythology? Certainly not, since, for him, "mythology" was a category that specifically distinguished such stories as those of Greek and Roman gods from biblical narratives. If we ask more bluntly, though, "Did Law think that there once was a single, in his case, androgynous, person who enjoyed living sinless on a paradisal Earth?" the answer is, most probably, yes. The problem, though, is the assumption that, for us, may accompany the question. The idea of "myth" opposed to "history" as "true" to "false" is hard

to shake, so we may think of Law as more hermeneutically innocent, as not enjoying the same level of sophisticated disillusion
as we do. It was, we may say with nostalgic sadness, "simpler"
for him. We come by this nagging prejudice quite honestly; modern culture, the culture much of which we share with Law and
within which he is in some ways a discordant and critical voice,
has privileged "literal" meaning over the metaphorical, symbolic,
or mythic. The latter have been held in not a little suspicion, as
"impure" or "emotional" as opposed to "rational." The connection with the "primitive" has further burdened mythological
expression. Thomas Hobbes, writing one of the foundational
works of modern political philosophy, tells us, therefore, that
"metaphors and other tropes" are forms of "inconstant" speech
and, as such, "can never be true grounds of any ratiocination."[12]
Or, as Thomas Sprat, in his history of the Royal Society, put it
triumphantly,

> The wit of the fables and religions of the ancient world
> is well-nigh consumed. They have already served the poets
> long enough, and it is high time to dismiss them.[13]

One of the many troubles to which this privileging of the "literal" leads is that it may well obscure an important commonality
that we do share with Law, a commonality that we can only
understand theologically. In a more profound way, though he did
believe that Adam was a "real person," Law knew perfectly well
that his descriptions of heaven, the angels, Adam, Eve, and Paradise were not "literally" true, that he could not *describe* such
things as they were. How so? As we have already noted frequently, Law takes the fall seriously. In his later writings we find
a cosmic account of the fall that is, if anything, even darker, more
horrifying. Fallenness is not a mote in the eye but rather a crossing and subverting of the power of sight itself, of our ability to see
at all. Fallen human beings are estranged from the knowledge of
God, which means that they do not see the world as it is — a point

that Law will make again and again. We do not know the world as God's good creation, the world as it is known and loved by God. Only the heart and mind reconciled and completely healed from sin know and love creation as it truly is, in its beauty, penetrated with the abundance of God, a mirror of the divine fullness. We have no "literal" knowledge of an unfallen world, no clear imagination of ourselves without the twist of sin, nothing but the dimmest sense of what it would be like to step from our hiding place and walk in a mild evening, unashamed with God. What we do have is Jesus, the perfect accommodation of God and humanity but within the terms of a world unhealed. For the home to which he leads us, for the new heaven and earth that he makes, for the depths of ruin that he repairs, for the change that he puts us to, we have the language of myth. This is a sense of "myth" that, applied to the Bible, goes beyond any secular definition and certainly would have been recognized by Law. Myth is our lisping before mystery, the words of those who are not yet free to praise otherwise, who have not yet entered a world in which everything is a radiant metaphor of God.

The Father's House

God Is Love

In his later writings Law expounds those "two great truths," our "deplorable condition" and the "new birth," in terms of a three-fold narrative scheme. I will follow this scheme through the final chapters of this book. Partly because of the special affection that he had for the parable, and partly to remind us of the Christ-centered character of his teaching, I have titled this and the final two chapters after moments in Jesus' parable of the prodigal son.[1] Law's narrative scheme involves a complex account of creation; a fall story that takes place in several stages and involves both angels and humanity; and a salvation narrative. The salvation narrative begins at the moment of humanity's fall, has its decisive turn in the incarnation, passion, and resurrection of Christ, and unfolds to final consummation through the work of the Spirit. Law's combining, expanding, and reinterpreting of the first three chapters of Genesis covers the first two parts of the scheme and the beginning of the third. This mythological narrative gives us the order of things, the economy of creation and fall, necessary to understanding God's way with Israel, the Son's incarnation, and the community of faith. We need to be alert to the complex relationship between the cosmic, social, and individual levels of this threefold scheme — that is, between "Jesus is what reality is about"; Israel and the church as the body of Christ; and Jesus as "*my* Lord and *my* God." The life and death of Jesus, for instance, is a decisive and unrepeatable event, unique in its universal signif-icance. It is also creative of a community that takes on the form of Christ. Within that community the individual lives of men and women recapitulate, through the Spirit and in their own particular way, Jesus' life and passion. The fall, too, is both universal in scope — a condition into which we are born, in some sense affecting the nonhuman as well as the human creation — and also a way we each follow for ourselves. As regards the three levels, Law attends rather less to the social level, that of the church, and more to the cosmic and individual. Not that he takes the church lightly, but all his writings, from *Christian Perfection* and *A Serious Call* onward, demonstrate his passion for a Christianity of the heart, a faith made interior in every Christian. He would hardly have denied, though, that the church is the formative context for such a faith.

The mythical narrative, upon which Law spends so much time, is really a cluster of myths. Nowhere does Law actually set it out all at once. Instead, the reader has to put the story together as, in the various dialogues and treatises, Law expounds one part or another. Before we consider the details, it is helpful, then, to follow the outline of the whole. Law's story begins not where Genesis begins but rather in eternity itself: in the love of Father, Son, and Spirit. The eternal expression of this love's glory is found in what Law calls "Eternal Nature." Out of the endless possibilities and powers of Eternal Nature, God creates the angels and their heavenly world. Darkness enters in, though, when some of the angels rebel, ruining themselves and also the part of heaven that is their gift and domain. God, however, prevents the endless maelstrom of their self-destruction by using the fiery ruins of their heaven as the material for a new creation, the temporal creation. So, the destructive power of the demonic is limited, trapped within the structure of this new creation, its darkness and harshness turned, taken up, and put to service in the new world. To populate this world, God creates Adam in his image and gives him the bliss of Paradise. Adam, though, is also blessed with the unstable gift of freedom, and soon he begins to love the creation rather than

God. He desires to know this Paradise as his *own* world, a world apart from God. In mercy, God splits this androgynous creature by creating, from out of Adam, Eve. Here is a creature whom Adam may love wholeheartedly and yet in doing so be referred constantly back to God through his image. Adam's fall, however, now Eve's as well, is completed in their disobedient choice of the "knowledge of good and evil," a choice that opens them to the darkness and the misery of insatiable desire. The story of redemption, however, begins precisely at this point. God does not leave them in their ruin but rather implants in them a "seed," an indwelling word of Christ, a persistent witness to the love that in Jesus will be fully made flesh.

God is love. This is the substance of Christian preaching, and Law, despite his critics, always held it at the core of his teaching. His later writings, however, expound this center and substance explicitly. Unlike in the practical treatises, for whose intended audience God's "love" was dangerously construed as God's "indulgence," when Law interprets Boehme, he brings the Divine love right into the foreground. God's "infinite Being," he celebrates,

> is an Infinity of mere Love, an unbeginning, never-ceasing, and forever overflowing Ocean of Meekness, Sweetness, Delight, Blessing, Goodness, Patience, and Mercy, and all this as so many blessed Streams breaking out of the Abyss of universal Love, Father, Son, and Holy Ghost, a Triune Infinity of Love and Goodness, for ever and ever giving forth nothing but the same Gifts of Light and Love, of Blessing and Joy, whether before or after the Fall, either of Angels or Men. (*SL* 423)

Terms tumble over each other as Law invokes a plentitude that our minds cannot encompass; we are caught up into images of flowing, expanding movement, "for ever and ever," in all directions, through time and across the orders of being. Law is trying to overwhelm us, deny us the ability to catch a tight hold of one idea or image. This literary strategy is clever and necessary. We find it both too difficult and too easy to think of God's love. Too difficult because we remember all the woes that appear to contradict it as well as all the awful things that Christians have thought compatible with this confession; too easy because "God is love" is sentimentalized, cheapened, trivialized, familiarized, and made generally compatible with some more or less constricted idea of our own good. Our thoughts need overwhelming here. We need the clichés shaken off us, and we need to realize that matters only get more difficult when we rush to measure God's love by our notions of what is and is not loving.

Still, if God is love, then we must say something because, at this point, silence would betray the reality of a love that constantly reaches out to us and finds its full statement in Jesus, who had good words as well as deeds for the wretched. In a very important sense, "God is love" is given content through the living of a Christian life. What this love means for us as adults is different from, though not necessarily better than, when we were children or in the midst of youthful experience. The intensities of joy, moments that are thrillingly graceful, life's gifts and unexpected delights, the examples and affection of others, as well as all those events that wrack us, oppose us, grieve us, our dying and the dying of others — the Spirit broods over all of it, imparting content, across our resistance, to "God is love." Even "the Wrath of an Enemy, the Treachery of a Friend, and every other Evil only helps the Spirit of Love to be more triumphant, to live its own Life and find all its own Blessings in a higher Degree" (*SL* 359).

Our individual experience of Divine love, though, is a sharing in Christ; it is part of the history in which God loved us before we loved God. Being loved by God means that, in the Spirit, our personal histories become his exegesis of Jesus, for whose history our lives are made commentary and praise. In our flesh and blood, even through all the layers of our frightful resistance, the Spirit interprets the Father's love, revealed in the Son. The story of Jesus, then, together with the history of Israel, of which it is the fulfillment, is the proper content of the confession "God is love." This is the love that came "first" and is now expounded in us. The cure for sentimentality, evasion, and naiveté is thus keeping before us the story of this love, from nativity to passion and resurrection. This desperately worldly, mortal, and temporal story is as such eternal because, as Law reminds us, God has never been anything other than what we see here, this vigorous life of love.

Here is the point: "God is love. God's love was revealed among us in this way: God sent his only Son into the world so that we might live through him" (1 John 4:8–9). There is no hidden side of God that stands in contradiction to what he did in sending his Son. There is no qualification to "God is love." That conviction is the root of Law's indignant denial that God should ever be referred to as "wrathful." God "can be nothing else but all Goodness toward [creation], because he can be nothing toward the Creature but that which he is, and was, and ever shall be in Himself" (*SL* 392). Nothing can "come to be" in God that is not eternally in God:

> Nothing that is *temporary, limited,* or bounded, can be in God. It is his Nature to be that which He is, and all that He is, in an infinite, unchangeable Degree. (*SL* 393)

God's love, therefore, is an "eternal immutable Will to all Goodness" (*SL* 393). Law interprets "love" in terms of will, but "wrath" he takes to be a "passion." "Wrath" is a passion from which arises the will for another's harm. To the extent that one is wrathful, one is not intending goodness. Clearly, if God is unequivocally loving and intends nothing but goodness, there is a contradiction here. It does not help if we simply say, "God's wrath is not like a human being's wrath." We need to provide some way of indicating where the difference lies, even though we will not be able to comprehend it. If we cannot do that, we suggest that the terms are equivocal —

that is, entirely unconnected with one another — and we are left
with a use of "wrath" to which we can assign no meaning. A
more promising path is to say that "wrath," when used of God,
functions as a metaphor conveying God's absolute opposition to
anything that opposes goodness — the resistance, as it were, inherent in his love's progress. At least in part, Law does take this
direction. He certainly uses "wrath" metaphorically. However,
since wrath is a passion, Law resists making God directly the object of the metaphor. Other passions he is happy to apply to God
metaphorically: sympathy, patience, faithfulness, for instance. All
these, however, may be grasped readily as modifications and forms
of love. "Wrath," in Law's view, cannot be understood as anything
other than a passion running counter to the "will to goodness,"
and therefore it is a contradiction to love, not a form of it. If
we predicate "wrath" of God, even metaphorically, we risk undermining Law's rule that God "can give nothing but Blessing,
Goodness, and Happiness from himself because he has in himself
nothing else to give" (*SL* 358). What Law does do, however, is
deploy the language of wrath as a metaphor for the consequences
of sin. "Wrath" gives us the "sinner's eye" view of a life in opposition to God's grace. Since Divine love does not compromise,
is unyieldingly intent on our good, resistance to it is experienced
as self-destruction. Goodness, joy, security, earthly love — in the
end, they all prove themselves impossible apart from God's love.
For the sinner, that impossibility is felt as "God's wrath." This
"wrath" is not in God, but the consequences of sin are just as
real.[2] A man who puts out his eyes may well say that the world
has become wholly dark, and indeed it has, yet the darkness is
not in the world but rather in the blindness that he has made.

"Eternal Nature" and the Triune God

God, then, is eternally loving, and, furthermore, this love is the
life of God as Father, Son, and Spirit. A consequence of this is

that God does not need the world in order to love — that is, to be God. From this it follows, too, that God is not dependent upon the world, and so, if there is a reality that is not God, this is entirely a matter of gift. The creation, therefore, does not need to be eternal but may have its own integrity as a finite, contingent reality of space and time. It is rather surprising to find, then, that having insisted upon the eternal Triune love, presumably with all that is supposed to follow from it, Law goes on to assert the existence of something called "Eternal Nature."

"Eternal Nature," Law tells us, is "an Infinity, or boundless opening of the properties, powers, wonders, and glories of the hidden Deity" (*SL* 418).[3] God knows his own wisdom, his own goodness, his own beauty, and Eternal Nature is the "opening," the infinite and eternal expression in which he knows it. Law identifies Eternal Nature, therefore, with God's "glory." All the possibilities, all the infinite variety of forms that God's command "Let there be" might realize or combine into creaturely being, are displayed in this garment of ideality. Eternal Nature is the dance of the Divine powers in which God raises and enjoys the inexhaustible energies of creation, all the ways in which he might give finite form to his wisdom, goodness, and beauty. "And this is not *once done*, but ever doing... for ever and ever breaking forth and springing up in new Forms and Openings of the abyssal Deity, in the Powers of Nature" (*SL* 46). God rejoices in this "outward Show" of "all the possible powers of life and glory," and from this eternal source, always "new Worlds of finite Divine Beings, as so many living Images of God... have a Possibility of coming forth" (*DK* 146).

The God whose life appears in these "living images" is the Triune God — Father, Son, and Spirit. How, then, does Eternal Nature manifest the unity and distinction of the persons of the Trinity? All reality, Law tells us, is an expression of the underlying dynamics of "fire, light, and spirit." These three, in their inter-relationship, constitute, first, the ideal forms of Eternal Nature, and then the existing, creaturely realities of heaven and earth. In the "first Workings of the *inconceivable God*" — Eternal Nature — God opens "his hidden Triune Deity in an outward State of Glory in the Splendour of united Fire, Light, and Spirit, all kindled and distinguished, all united and beatified by the *hidden Three*" (*DK* 114). At first blush, we seem to be quite distant from the narrative within which the Triune God is revealed: the story of Jesus, sent by the God of Israel, whom he calls "Abba," to bind all things to himself in the Holy Spirit. "Fire," "light," and "spirit," however, all have ample biblical precedent. "Fire" is a familiar image for Israel's God, "light" is used to identify Jesus in the New Testament, and "Spirit" is what is given in consequence of what occurs between the Father and Jesus. Hence, "God hath sent forth the Spirit of his Son into your hearts, crying, Abba, Father" (Gal. 4:6). Interpreting Law's account, we need to attend especially to the way the elements of fire, light, and spirit are related to one another, forming a "threefold life" of unity-in-diversity. This follows the classical Trinitarian rule that the persons are distinguished by their relations to one another and not by their divinity, which is one and the same. We must remember, too, that, as constituting elements of creation, "fire, light, spirit" are images, manifestations in nondivine reality of the inconceivable Mystery. They present, therefore, a similarity, but one that exists within an always greater dissimilarity.

In *An Appeal to All That Doubt,* Law sets out the unity and distinction, the relations involved in creation's triune correspondence to its Creator. He does this with a straightforwardness that is more apparent than real:

> The kingdom of heaven stands in this threefold life, where three are one, because it is a manifestation of the Deity, which is three and one; the Father has his distinct manifestation in the fire, which is always generating the light; the Son has his distinct manifestation of the light, which is

always generated from the fire; the Holy Ghost has his manifestation in the spirit, that always proceeds from both, and
is always united with them.[4]

"Spirit" appears the odd one out here. "Fire" and "light" are
material entities, while "spirit" surely is not. Also, we can readily
understand that a fire produces light, but what are we to make of
"spirit" proceeding from both, "united with them," and, presumably, uniting them? Fire and light, though, are not simply material
realities in Law's view. Certainly, they both take material forms
in, for example, the fire in the grate and the light from the sun,
but these are only instances of two powers that have their ideal
forms in Eternal Nature and are actual throughout creation as
the powers of life and of harmonious order, connectedness, and
beauty. So, Law claims,

> Fire has but *one Nature* through the whole Universe of
> Things, and material Fire has not more or less of the Nature
> of Fire in it, than that which is in eternal Nature; because
> it has nothing, works nothing, but what it has, and works
> from thence. (*SL* 383)

There are, therefore, the fire that is the life in animate things and
the light that is understanding. There can also be fire without
light, and in a fallen world the fire that constitutes the total life
of an individual person may be a dark fire, a fire without the light
that is God's illumining of the mind and heart.

If one presses the question of what exactly "fire, light, spirit"
mean here and how are they mutually implicated in a threefold
life, then Law is not altogether helpful, leaving his readers to join
the dots for themselves. "Fire" must be sorted out first and, especially, Law's peculiar claim that fire "has but *one Nature* through
the whole Universe of Things." In 1752, the physician and re-
searcher John Freke sent Law a copy of his recently published
work on electricity.[5] Freke had found gratifying parallels between

Law's remarks on fire in *The Spirit of Love* and the speculations that he based on his own experiments. Since Law acknowledged the coincidence of ideas, we may look to Freke for some help in interpreting Law. Freke's treatises on fire and on electricity, which he calls "agitated fire," give this element a fundamental role in the cosmos. Our routine commerce with fire, in cooking or warming ourselves, gives us no idea of fire's true nature or importance, a point made in a similar fashion by Law. We need to realize that fire comes in many forms that are but modifications of this element.[6] There is fire "impacted" in flints and in "many other hard stones and metals," and it is dispersed in particles throughout the air, which, breathed in by animals or absorbed by plants, ignites and maintains life.[7] Fire is, therefore, the energy of life. Freke encourages us, somewhat heartlessly, to prove this at the small expense of a candle and a cat. Lock them both in an airtight space such as an oven, and both will expire at the same moment. Reckless of both pets and logic, Freke thinks this demonstrates that, since the cat and candle both go out when they have used up all the air, it is the fire in the air that generates both life and flame. Exceeding even the sphere of organic nature, fire is everywhere the "principal and first cause of activity and motion."[8] Fire holds all things in their proper movement, "as well in Animals, as Vegetables and Minerals." Deprived of it, entities fall apart and dissolve. Fire is the power through which creatures assert themselves in their particular integrity as living realities. Law finds a similar theory in his reading of Boehme, and so fire becomes the image in finitude of God the Father as eternal energy and source of deity.

Thankfully, in connection with "light" and "spirit," Law allows the force of biblical imagery to determine more closely the range of meanings. He associates "light" very closely with "love," so that the phrase "Light and Love" appears routinely. Eternal Nature itself consists of nothing other than the "Forms of triumphing Light and Love" (*SL* 364). The logic of this derives

from Law's understanding of Jesus and is exemplified particularly, though by no means solely, in John's Gospel, where Jesus is
"the light of the world" who reveals the Father's love (John 8:12;
cf. 3:16; 17:21–26). Nothing can quench the fretful longings of
creatures except "that same heavenly Light and Love which was
made Flesh to redeem the fallen Humanity first, and after that the
whole material System" (*SL* 377). The coincidence of light and
love allows Law to read Genesis 1 in its terms:

> And as Light thus brought forth is *the first State* that is *lovely*
> and *delightful* in Nature, so the Spirit of Love has only its
> Birth *in the Light* of Life, and can be nowhere else. For
> the Properties of Life have no *common Good*, nothing to
> rejoice in, till the Light is found; and therefore no possible
> Beginning of the Spirit of Love till then. (*SL* 384)

Light is the original beauty given to creation and the possibility of all other beauties, since light constitutes and reveals them:
from colors and shapes to perception and wisdom. The refrain in
Genesis 1, "and God saw that it was good," corresponds to the
original, "Let there be light." All the goodness of creation and all
knowledge and delight in that goodness depend upon the original
gift of light. As the first gift that makes all other gifts possible,
light is the first act of love toward creation and makes creation a
"*common* Good." On the one hand, this light, which reveals the
world as Divine gift, is the finite "manifestation" of the eternal
Son, the light through whom God the Father knows and delights
in his own life. On the other hand, created light is the prophetic
sign of that same Son, who, when humanity chose darkness and
chaos, reprises and exceeds the creative gift in giving himself as
enduring light "to the first fallen Man, as *a Seed of the* Woman,
as a *Light* of Life, *enlightening every Man that comes into the
World*" (*SL* 448; cf. John 1:9).

Biblical themes also dominate Law's thoughts on "spirit."
What he has to say about the Holy Spirit, the Spirit of God,

determines the meaning of created spirit and its ideal form in Eternal Nature. Creation participates in the Divine life through the Holy Spirit, who is God lifting up and enclosing his beloved creation within the communion of Father, Son, and Spirit. Where the Spirit is, there is the heavenly life of God:

> And as the Deity, Father, Son, and Holy Spirit, are always in Heaven, and make Heaven to be everywhere, so this Spirit, breathed by them into Man, brought Heaven into Man along with it. (*SP* 4)

The Holy Spirit, therefore, quickens the dead and reconciles the separated, keeping "the Soul fixed, and continually turned towards God." The inspiration of the Spirit, without which "nothing can turn to God, desire to be united to him, and governed by him," is not external to our "spirit," a force acting upon it. Rather, the Holy Spirit is the "spirit" of our lives insofar as they are united with God and yearn for God. "Every Prayer for the Holy Spirit, *is the Spirit itself praying in you*" (*SP* 115 [my emphasis]). When Law's straight man, Academicus, finally catches on, he is able to explain,

> My own good Spirit is the Breath of God in me, and so related to God, as the Breath of my animal Life is related to the Air. . . . It is from God, has the Nature, the Eternity, the Spirituality of God, as the Breath of my Flesh and Blood, has the Grossness, the earthly, transitory Nature of the Spirit of this World. (*SP* 139)

"Spirit," then, is what unites us to an environment, either the eternal, heavenly one or that of the fallen world. This is very important. Spirit is not something that we *possess*; spirit encloses, penetrates, possesses us, joining us to a larger life. The angels, who thus "live, move, and have their Being in God" (*SP* 62), share in the Divine vision of Eternal Nature, enthralled as "new Scenes in the Mirror of Divine Wisdom" (*SP* 62) appear, connect, and change. To put it slightly differently: spirit is what makes a collection of creatures into an ecosystem, and a mob of men and women into the *body* of Christ. As creatures, we belong to an environment, and about that we have no choice. The issue is whether we are conformed to the closed, ultimately illusory, environment of the fallen world or taken up within the infinitely open ecology of the Trinity.

First, then, we have "Holy Spirit," uniting the Father and the Son, quickening the dead, forming the church at Pentecost: the infinite loop, relay, connectivity, and community of the living. Created spirit, which constitutes the bonds of Nature giving us "Nature" rather than a mere heap of beings, is the finite manifestation, medium, and image of Holy Spirit. Finally, there is "the spirit of this world" because the "world" is also an environment, an ecology of destruction. This, too, however perverted and corrupt, cannot but be also an image of true and Holy Spirit. If light spreads, discloses, and reveals, spirit unites and gathers into complex wholes. We are now closer to understanding Law's claim that all reality is an expression of those underlying dynamics of "fire, light, spirit" that manifest the Trinity. Insofar as creation realizes the Divine vision in Eternal Nature, the substance, integrity, distinct being of things, their self-assertion or "fire" opens out as light and love, making creatures good and beautiful in the sphere to which they give themselves, as the "spirit" unifies them with and within their environment. This threefold movement manifests the Triune God. The Father does not hoard up being but rather generates the Son, in whom all things are created, and the mutual return of love that is the Spirit unites them and all that the Son incorporates.

Law attempted the difficult task, especially difficult in the theological climate of the eighteenth century, of making faith in the Trinity count. He tries to read creation as the creation of the Triune God, whose eternal life of love is disclosed right to the very fibers of the world. God — Father, Son, and Spirit — generating, receiving, offering, proceeding, and binding, is, Law insists, "the very form, and beauty, and brightness" of creation (*SP* 46). Law's way of going about this is not always clear, and he further muddies the business in the *Spirit of Love* when he expands the threefold "fire, light, spirit" to accommodate Boehme's doctrine of the "seven properties." More seriously, mention of the Trinity is often oriented to cosmology rather than to the Word made flesh or the Holy Spirit in the church. This tends to obscure the grounding of Trinitarian confession, including Law's, in biblical narrative rather than philosophical reflection. Also, in relation to both creation and redemption, Law leaves the distinction of the Trinitarian persons underdeveloped.[9] In fairness, though, we should remember that Law is writing not a systematic theology but rather what he understands as *practical* theology — that is, works that work, that move the will through which God's formation and sanctification of us proceed.

The key point is that Law does attempt this important task of thinking in terms of the Trinity. Rejection of Trinitarian doctrine by such as the Deists was very much a minority position in the eighteenth century. Nevertheless, though generally adhered to, the confession of God as Father, Son, and Spirit was hardly formative for either theology or practice. Anglican liturgy might still be thoroughly Trinitarian, but sermons, books of moral guidance, and works of devotion pay it relatively little mind. Those who do address the subject largely, if unintentionally, confirm that the doctrine is, in practice, of marginal significance. John Tillotson, who became archbishop of Canterbury in 1691, took up the cause of Trinitarian belief as both scholar and preacher. In *A Seasonable Vindication of the Blessed Trinity*, Tillotson argues that God may and has revealed truths that are "above" reason. These truths are beyond our comprehension but still rational to believe, given the authority of Scripture and that God, being "infinitely good and faithful, cannot deceive us."[10] He argues the scriptural case for the Trinity, and that the doctrine amounts to neither a logical contradiction nor belief in three gods, before finishing up by rejecting any parallel between belief in the Trinity and belief in transubstantiation. There is no attempt to show why the belief matters and no indication that it might belong to the inner logic of Christian faith, shaping that faith all the way down. Instead, we find argument for a doctrinal proposition that appears to stand pretty well by itself as an odd, if obscurely important, fact about God. Tillotson's published sermon "Concerning the Unity of the Divine Nature and the Blessed Trinity" covers much the same ground and is little better in locating the doctrine's importance. His concluding "application" simply argues that acknowledging God's Son as the one who suffered for us should make us more keen in repentance and persistent in obedience.[11] Certainly, confession of Jesus' divine sonship is a key provocation of Trinitarian faith, but Tillotson's point does not arise directly from that faith, nor does he even hint as to how creation, church, redemption, sanctification, prayer, or practice might bear a particular shape because a Triune God is at the center of it all. In the rough and tumble of controversy with the Deists, Trinitarian doctrine suffers a similar fate. Anti-Deist works, such as James Foster's attempt to rebut Matthew Tindal, are all too happy to fight the battle on the enemy's territory, accept the Deist's terms of engagement, and argue that my God is more reasonable than your God.[12] The doctrine of the Trinity was left politely on the margins, if mentioned at all.

Giving the Deist Humanus a strictly nonspeaking part in the dialogues of *The Spirit of Prayer* may be a peculiar device, but it does underscore Law's refusal to observe the terms of contemporary debate. Humanus has to hear the gospel speak for itself and not filtered through questions that, because they are set by its critics, carry their underlying assumptions as to the character of the gospel. Humanus "has never yet been in Sight of the Truth, as it is in the Gospel; he knows nothing of the Grounds and Reason of it" (*SL* 61), though he has read the books of controversy. Tillotson and others defended the doctrine of the Trinity as a set of propositions that are "very rational" to believe and should be accepted either on the ground of biblical and church authority or through rational exegesis that demonstrated the sound basis of that authority. Law, however, will not reduce God's revelation to the passivity of propositions offered for intellectual debate. He would not accept so mealy-mouthed an account of God's truth, for "when rightly understood," this truth is not merely credible, it is "irresistible" (*SP* 61)! In the light of the state of theology in the early eighteenth century, Law's attempt to show the vitality of naming God as Father, Son, and Spirit is quite remarkable. God's Triune being, he argues, determines the form of all that God does and everything that God creates. Something clearly had gone awry, since awareness of this had become so attenuated that the Trinity was now reduced to the object of a rather isolated and merely intellectual assent.

When the curtain goes up on the drama of Law's narrative, we see Eternal Nature, the play of God's eternal wisdom, "daily his delight, rejoicing always before him" (Prov. 8:30). The "majestic presence of the abysmal, unsearchable, triune God" is visible in the glory of his wisdom, the "workshop" of his creativity.[13] This beginning of the myth shows us a "communicative" God, a God who is eternally generating and receiving the life of Triune love and who eternally delights to make that life known. Eternal Nature is the vision of divine fecundity and generosity. Law has to be careful here, however. He does not, as we will see, want to represent creation itself as eternal, nor is Eternal Nature divine "stuff" out of which the world is made. The point of Eternal Nature is not to blur the distinction between God and the creation in the direction of pantheism. Creation can be the free gift of love that Law insists it is only if the world is not eternally given along with or as part of God's being. God does not "need" to create, as if he required the project for self-fulfillment. Nor does God owe us being. To be is gift. On the other hand, the concept of Eternal Nature tells us that there is nothing arbitrary about the universe that God creates. This goes to the heart of Law's cosmic and redemptive vision: creation is the working of God, making himself manifest in and through what is other than himself. Our world, and we within it, are eternally prepared beforehand in those forms through which God spreads out his Wisdom and in which the Father, Son, and Spirit celebrate their mutual love in the expression of an inexhaustible fruitfulness. If this is Eternal Nature and the "deep and true ground of all things" (*DK* 114), then the world that we inhabit, tragically marred though it is, is a creation in which we may recognize the Triune God. None of the many ways in which we read the world through all the sciences — natural, human, and social — and none of the meanings that imagination finds in the world are capable of exhausting it. In its immensities and in its merest threads, God is "breaking forth into visibility" (*DK* 145). The figure of Eternal Nature announces the God who delights to speak, and it secures the world's enduring openness and readability.

This brings us back, perhaps surprisingly, to the practical concerns of *A Serious Call* and *Christian Perfection*. *A Serious Call* is an exhortation to change, and change belongs to the integrity of a Christian life. The goal of that change is the principal theme of *Christian Perfection*. Both treatises insist over and over again that they are addressing not a spiritual elite but rather all Christians. If we appeal to our churchgoing regularity, to Jesus' death, or to "justification by faith alone" as excuses for not changing, we mistake God's grace for cheap grace. God is not satisfied until he sees us as he intended us in the beginning. Eternal Nature grounds the uncompromising demands of the practical treatises in God's eternity, in our form manifested in the play of Wisdom.

> Let no man therefore trust to be saved at the last day, by any arbitrary goodness, or free [i.e., cheap] grace of God;

...salvation can be found by no creature but by its own full...concurring with those mysterious means, which the free grace of God hath afforded for the recovery of our first, perfect, glorious state in nature.[14]

Again, Law turns the Deists' own language against them. Rigorous they may be, but any requirements that serve Christian perfection are, for that reason, far from arbitrary. They are rooted in Nature itself, not that dull clockwork that Deists took for Nature but rather in Nature seen eternally in the glorious counsel of the Trinity. With the doctrine of Eternal Nature, then, Law is also indirectly staking out his own position within the eighteenth-century debates on Nature. Undoubtedly, this position helped earn him his contemporary reputation for what today we would term "kookiness."

Creation or Clockwork?

By the early eighteenth century, Nature had turned into a machine. Mathematics and mechanics appeared as the "alphabet, in which God wrote the world."[15] The philosophical, the scientific, and, to all intents and purposes, the rational approaches to nature were to consider it as a mechanism, a system of material relations, of action and reaction according to the laws of motion. Law's admirer John Freke, therefore, could announce to his readers that he would "first suppose that the world is a machine" and add that the supposition was so obvious that "no reasonable man can doubt it." The mechanistic account of the natural world had not enjoyed such hegemonic status for very long. Early modern technology may seem very limited to us, but the seventeenth-century English had enjoyed an unprecedented increase in technological innovation. Systems of irrigation were improved; gears were widely used in mills; cranes and lifting devices bore heavier loads; pistons, pumps, and new furnaces aided expanding mining and metallurgical industries; barometers and thermometers made scientific research more precise; and precision clocks and the spiral balance spring gave new orderliness to time.[16] An expanding commercial economy favored mechanization, encouraged technological development, and, in turn, provided a framework of plausibility for the ready appropriation of mechanistic theories of nature.[17]

Robert Boyle's *Free Enquiry into the Vulgarly Received Notion of Nature*, published in 1686, is a founding document for mechanism. Boyle attacks traditional ideas of nature as a living body, as an organic host to innumerable lives, itself animated by "spirit." He argues that these notions, which he also caricatures, are empty fancies that obstruct science and that, in ascribing formative powers to nature, take away honor due God as sole creator. Nature is, rather, a "compounded machine," like a ship. "Such an engine as comprises or consists of several lesser engines." In the beginning, diverse motions separated matter into forms of greater and lesser bulk and shape. Once all parts of this inanimate vastness settled into place, their future operations were strictly governed by the laws of motion.

> Though men talk of nature as they please, yet whatever is done among things inanimate . . . is really done but by particular bodies acting on one another by local motion, modified by the other mechanical affections of the agent, of the patient, and of those other bodies that necessarily concur to the effect or the phenomenon produced.[18]

On more cautious days, Boyle acknowledged that some phenomena, such as gravity, eluded mechanical explanation. In *A Free Enquiry*, though, his enthusiasm triumphs.

This enthusiasm was as much religious as scientific. The "great construction" witnessed to the glory and wisdom of God, and since nature was an inanimate machine, we owed devotion, regard, and thanks to God alone. Even so, in this text by a very devout Christian there are signs of disturbing problems inherent in the "mechanical philosophy." Boyle is awed by God's immense contrivance, but the reduction of nature to a mechanical complex also robbed it of wonder. Boyle confesses to a narrowing of human knowledge, that it is limited to, as he puts it tellingly, "a small (not to say contemptible) portion" of reality. He wonders if all "the powers and effects of matter and motion" might turn out not to be no more than "an epicycle" in God's grand scheme. He longs for the heavenly day when God will give greater things as the object of human research and "enlarge our faculties" for it.[19] Mechanism, though, also raised very uncomfortable questions for human life itself. Boyle's older contemporary Thomas Hobbes had already attempted to account for the human mind in purely materialistic and mechanical terms. This horrified Boyle, who insists on the uniqueness of human beings as having immortal and immaterial souls, welded though they are to our bodily "engines." His vehemence, though, evidences the seriousness of the problem. If all nature, including our bodies, may be explained mechanically, what price the soul? Was humanity the image of God, wandering among the cogs and wheels or, perhaps, just another part of the machine, no more free or eternal than plankton? Finally, if the world was a properly contrived machine, did it need the benefit of Divine servicing? Even an ideal machine cannot create itself, perhaps, but once started, it should manage without further help. Boyle argued that God's continued action in nature was needed. Without his active power, everything would fly apart according to the first law of motion. Boyle even defended miracles. Yet, delight in the machine can get the better of him:

> [The world] 'tis like a rare Clock, such as may be that at *Strasbourg*, where all things are so skillfully contriv'd, that the Engine being once set a moving, all things proceed according to the Artificers first design, and the motions...do not require...the peculiar interposing of the Artificer, or any

Intelligent Agent employed by him, but perform their functions upon particular occasions, by virtue of the General and Primitive contrivance of the whole Engine.[20]

Boyle's language here slips far toward the very Deism that Law identifies as a theology for worldliness.

The technological and theoretical benefits of the mechanical model have been huge. Its dangers derive from the degree to which our culture has taken the metaphor for the reality, reducing both nature and humanity to the terms of the model and obscuring creation's vast remainder. Whereas Boyle still retained a sense of the model's limits, of what it could not account for, the mechanical philosophy took increasingly more dogmatic forms as it penetrated Western culture. Right up to the mid-twentieth century, "the paradigm of the clockwork universe was still very much alive," persisting through fundamental scientific challenges going back as far as research into thermodynamics in the early nineteenth century.[21] Consequently, despite developments from quantum to chaos theories, the mechanistic physics that triumphed in the seventeenth century remains the "common-sense" account of things.[22] The model's endurance, however, has as much to do with its cultural role as anything else. The mechanistic outlook rationalized the domination and exploitation of nature, degrading nature to a lifeless object of exploitation. Extended into economics, social theory, and politics, mechanistic theories made the rule-governed, predictable, and socially conformist aspects of human beings the most interesting thing about them. The human consequences, from the absorption of individuals into the factory system to mass murder according to the laws of genetics or history, continue to horrify us and intimate future darkness.

Law does not take on mechanistic theory directly. His vision, however, exposes its limitations. He shows us how any adequate account of God's creation bursts the constraints of mechanical reductionism or, for that matter, of any deterministic, totalizing theory, from evolution to information, that reduces the world to one or other set of immanent processes. Newton's "*three* great Laws of *Matter* and *Motion*," Law observes, are "so much celebrated" as not to need further applause. What, however, is their true significance?

> In the mathematical System of this great Philosopher these three Properties, *Attraction*, equal *Resistance*, and the *orbicular Motion* of the Planets as the effect of them, *&c.*, are only treated of as *Facts* and *Appearances*. (SL 375)

The mechanical philosophy does not get to the root or, as Law would say, the "ground" of the movements that it theorizes. There is no doubt as to its usefulness. The mapping of mechanism provided a stabilized account of the energies of creation. It rendered the interlocking acting and reacting forces in a form favorable to the advance of human power and instrumental control of the environment. Less happily, it also spawned some rather complacent apologies for evil such as Pope's

> All chance, direction, which thou canst not see;
> All discord, harmony not understood;
> All partial evil, universal good
> ... One truth is clear; Whatever *Is*, is *Right*."[23]

To think that the model represents reality in its depth, however, is to betray oneself to "facts and appearances." Behind these "facts and appearances," these forces domesticated for our comprehension, is their reality as spiritual events in material form. Nature is no dead mechanism. As Law warns, "there are no dead Forms, or lifeless Inventions to be found, till you come to the mechanic Works of Men's Hands, and the cobweb Schemes of dead Knowledge, brought forth by human Reason" (DK 163). Law's world is saturated with divine purpose and history. When we pass from "facts and appearances" to the world as it hangs upon the possibilities of God, we are like two-dimensional creatures suddenly surprised into a three-dimensional world.

Boyle's "elaborate engine" is a closed system, its movements predictable, determined, and prior to the acknowledgment of entropy, essentially sufficient unto its own continuance.[24] Not so, says Law; such equilibrium is only apparent. Creation's dynamics are a restless striving beyond the present condition of things, a "Working and Strife after a *Unity* and *Purity* which it can neither have nor forbear to seek" (*SL* 364). The world is in travail, groaning for a future from the hand of God (Rom. 8:20–25). This is an "open" creation, an as yet unfinished, laboring creation. From the machine-universe one might deduce the power and contriving wisdom of God, but only a vision that takes up nature and humanity into a single sweep of Divine yearning can recognize creation as the workshop of Divine love:

> The Almighty brought forth all Nature for this only End, that boundless Love might have its *Infinity* of Height and Depth to dwell and work in, and all the striving and working Properties of Nature are only to give *Essence* and *Substance*, Life and Strength, to the *invisible hidden Spirit of Love*, that it may come forth into outward Activity. (*SL* 366)

Creation is thus open to the action of God, not the odd tinkering miracle that Boyle and others were prepared to accept, but rather a constant "working will," a history in which God raises up new possibilities in defiance of all that deforms the makings of his love.

As we saw, the mechanical philosophy either drove a wedge between humanity and nature, rendering the human mind alien to its bodily engine, or resolved the opposition reductively, making the mind, too, a product of local motions. However, if God's action is a single story, if all nature is expressive of spirit, then there must be a vital continuity between humanity and nature. "Body and Spirit, therefore, are not two *separate, independent* Things, but are *necessary* to each other, and are only the *inward* and *outward* conditions of *one* and the *same Being*" (*SL* 372). Spirit is no stranger to matter; matter is its outward form, its manifestation. Only because of this can we recognize that Nature's calling is as "a Birth or Manifestation of the triune invisible Deity."

Law hangs all these convictions upon the doctrine of Eternal Nature, "the first Manifestation, the first Opening of the Divine Omnipotence." "All that God is, and can do, or bring forth from himself, is done in and by the working of his Triune Spirit in this eternal Nature" (*DK* 114). The Triune God creates out of the eternal play of his Wisdom; what *is* proceeds from the Divine glory. This is the huge remainder to which the machine-universe leaves no witness. Nature is plotted by God, and so Nature's eternal ideal, dissatisfaction, disease, and groaning penetrate into the very roots of a fallen world. All things must become transparent to glory. Nature itself, and not humanity alone, has a vocation precisely because God never envisaged human beings without a world. Humanity is not redeemed alone; there is no perfection for the human save that nature is perfected too, realizing the vision of Eternal Nature.

Eternal Nature is the beginning before the beginning. Out of Eternal Nature the Triune God elects the creation that he will summon through his Son and Word: "Let there be. . . . " The first summoning is of the angelic world. Heaven and the events that occur in heaven commence the drama of fall and redemption. Before we turn to the angels, though, we must notice that it is at this point that Law squabbles with one of the most enduring of classical Christian doctrines. According to the consensus of most Christian traditions before Law's time and since, God created the heavens and the earth "out of nothing." This doctrine is often referred to in its Latin form as the doctrine of *creatio ex nihilo*. Exact biblical warrant for the doctrine is a little thin. Law's English Bible, the King James translation, offers Hebrews 11:3 thus:

Through faith we understand that the worlds were framed
by the word of God, so that things which are seen were not
made of things which do appear.[25]

A clearer point of biblical contact is found in a book deemed
apocryphal by Protestants, 2 Maccabees: "Look upon the heaven
and the earth, and all that is therein, and consider that God made
them of things that were not" (2 Macc. 7:28). The importance
of the doctrine derived, then, not from clear biblical reference.
As much as anything else, creation "out of nothing" is a necessary teaching because the alternatives are quite unacceptable.
Creation *ex nihilo* denied both that God created an eternal and
divine world out of his own "substance," an essentially pantheist solution, and that he created out of some preexisting matter,
a possibility that denied the ultimacy of God as sole ground of
all being. The classical Christian position became that creation
is an absolute gift. God did not have to create; he filled no lack
in doing so, needed no help in doing so. Moreover, the creation,
thereby, has its own integrity and relative independence; it is not
illusion or mere appearance but rather is real, with all the reality and integrity needed to be the object of love. Youth workers
who insist on teaching that ghastly song with the line "merrily,
merrily, merrily, merrily, life is but a dream" might do well to remember that they are inducting the innocent into one of the most
fundamental of heresies.

William Law would not deny any of this. He had no quarrel
with Newton's warning that "we are not to consider the world as
the body of God, or the several parts thereof, as parts of God."[26]
Law was no pantheist; the reality of creation is essential to everything that he says, and he gives no ground for denying creation
as absolute gift. So why does he have a problem with creation
ex nihilo if that is what the doctrine has always meant? The
easy answer would be to say that, for him, creation was not
"from nothing" but rather "from Eternal Nature." The latter,

however, is a way of affirming that God is sole origin of all creation, containing beforehand all its perfections in his own Triune
life. Claiming that creation manifests the Divine glory and eternal Wisdom does not contradict creation *ex nihilo*. It is perfectly
possible, given the classical understanding of "out of nothing,"
to affirm both. The weaker suggestion, though, that Law simply
preferred "from Eternal Nature" or thought it more adequate is
not satisfying either, since Law rejects creation "out of nothing"
so vehemently. "It is a *Fiction*," he fumes, "big with the grossest
Absurdities" (*SP* 75). At one level, Law's fury is a waste of energy,
since he is misreading the classical doctrine. On occasion, he even
finds a simple contradiction here as if centuries of theological reflection had not noticed that, as King Lear put it, "nothing can
come of nothing."

More seriously, Law regards "from nothing" as an implicit
denial that God in any way gives himself or manifests himself in
creation:

> ["Out of nothing"] *separates* every thing from God, it leaves
> *no Relation* between God and the Creature, nor any *Possi-
> bility* for any *Power, Virtue, Quality,* or *Perfection* of God,
> to be in the Creature: for if it is created *out of nothing*, it
> cannot have *something* of God in it. (*SP* 76)

This shows us what Law is fighting for. He sees *ex nihilo* as a
denial that the creation has any precedent, any rootedness in the
Divine life. If the world comes "from nothing," he reasons, then
it reflects nothing, manifests nothing beyond its own appearance.

> If that which begins to be comes out of Nothing, it can only
> have the Nature of that out of which it comes; and therefore
> can have no more said about it, why it is this or that, than
> can be said of that Nothing, from whence it comes. (*DK* 248)

Indeed, nothing does come of nothing, and a creation "from nothing" can "bear no testimony of God." In other words, if this

creation has no precedent within the life of God, such as is given through Eternal Nature, then the character of the world, that it is this world rather than another, is entirely *arbitrary.* That is the key term. In debates over the rationalist theology of the Deists, "natural" and "arbitrary" were fundamental and opposing categories. The God who calls a particular people, sends his Son, and demands faith in Jesus' saving work is an "arbitrary" God, whereas the God who demands only that we act according to what we can reason out for ourselves is behaving "according to nature," and his religion is "natural." Law appears to have taken the Deist understanding of the creation as a self-contained rational system and read that back into the classical doctrine of creation *ex nihilo*, a doctrine that, indeed, Deists accepted. Since he is determined to seize the opposition natural/arbitrary and turn it back on the Deists, he rejects the arbitrariness that he associates with creation "out of nothing." Although Law has misunderstood the classical doctrine, his misunderstanding, given the theological context, stands for something important. The mechanical creation — creation brought within the horizon of instrumental rationality — is, for all the appearance of intelligibility, an enigma that only refers back to itself. The gospel, by contrast, finds the world significant, even though one can read the signs only by following the way of the cross. There is nothing arbitrary about creation because there is nothing arbitrary about love. Christians read the world as the manifestation of God's love, the love at one with eternal Wisdom that knows everything before it was anything.

"In the beginning, God created the heavens. . . . " God makes a choice; out of all the possibilities of Eternal Nature, God elects, first, the creation of the angelical kingdom, and second, the temporal creation of which we are part. In doing this, God commits his Word, his faithfulness, not just generally but rather to a particular history. There is no going back. Not that there could not be, but that God chooses that there should not be: he chooses faithfulness that is, as God well knows, the way of the cross. The

Lamb is slain before the creation of the world. This point becomes clearer if we think about the alternative, rather creepily imagined in Greg Bear's science fiction classic, *Blood Music.* An experiment in marrying DNA with computer technology results in the creation of intelligent cells that bring about the final stage in universal evolution. Initially passed like a virus, the cells multiply by the trillion to form cellular societies that first transform their human hosts and then the material world itself. These "noocytes" dismantle reality and reencode it as information that they can research and manipulate. The end of their exploring is the realization of material reality as "noosphere." In the "noosphere" everything that is, has been, or possibly could be is retained and made available as information, combinable in inexhaustibly varied forms. The noosphere is thus able to reproduce the lives of the novel's main characters in endlessly different versions as well as generate pockets of consciousness to experience them. No past is fixed and no opportunities are lost, since every possible history may be configured, dismantled, and reconfigured in the noosphere. The novel ends with this refrain: "Nothing is lost. Nothing is forgotten. / It was in the blood, the flesh, / And now it is forever."[27]

There are some obvious similarities between Bear's "noosphere" and William Law's "Eternal Nature." A crucial difference, of course, is that Eternal Nature is encompassed by transcendent love, the mystery of the Triune God, whereas the noosphere is the whole of reality. Bear's vision is "monist." The most important thing to notice about the noosphere is that Bear represents it as the fulfillment of human and, indeed, universal reality. The characters go quite gently into their noospheric dissolution. As one character passes into the informational world, he writes,

> [The noocytes] are the grand achievement. They love. They cooperate. They have discipline, yet are free; they know death but are immortal.

They now know me thru and thru. I am a theme in their art, their wonderful living "fictions." They have duplicated me a million times over. Which of me writes this? I do not know. There is no longer an original.

I can go off in a million directions, lead a million lives (. . . in Thought, Imagination, Fantasy!) and then gather my selves together, hold a conference, and start all over again.

. . . Paul, I wish you could join us.[28]

In the noosphere nothing is lost — except loss itself. That, however, is to lose precisely the glory and tragedy of creation. In creating, God commits himself to the irrevocable, to particular being, to the creative decision for this and not that, to a history that may be redeemed but not unmade. Creation, as Christians understand it, is God's irrevocable commitment to particular being. God's faithfulness begins in his choice of a creation that cannot be recalled, in which losses are real, the stakes are high, and in which the resurrected Christ bears forever the marks of crucifixion.

The Way into the Far Country

The Fall of Angels

First, God creates the angels and their angelic kingdoms. Law moves the mythical narrative quickly on from this creation to the initial tragedy of rebellion and ruin. He does, though, offer us one glimpse of angelic life before disaster fell. Their heavenly kingdom is described as having the "materiality" of a "glassy sea." This glass sea is the medium in which the angels dwell. The figure of the "glass sea" has its biblical origins in the book of Revelation. John sees the throne of God:

> And before the throne there was a sea of glass like unto crystal: and in the midst of the throne, and round about the throne, were four beasts full of eyes before and behind.
>
> (Rev. 4:6 [cf. 15:2])[1]

Jacob Boehme had picked up the image, describing the glass sea as "the seventh property of the eternal nature . . . whence this world was created into sundry peculiar heavens and forms."[2] Law develops the associations of "glass" rather than of "sea," though the sea does suggest the boundlessness and perhaps also the mobility of the angelic world. "Glass" is treated as a transparency, a spiritual medium through which the angels continually enjoy the wonders of God as they "open and change." Alternatively, a mirror is indicated upon which "beauteous Forms, Figures, Virtues, Powers, Colours, and Sounds, which were perpetually springing up, [are] appearing and changing in an infinite Variety" (SP 10).

118

As Law uses the glass sea also to describe the final reconciled heaven and earth, the image is an important one. The Triune life is one in which the persons are eternally "transparent" to one another. In their mutual love, there is no hoarding, no retreat from one another, no hiding such as occurs when Adam and Eve first break fellowship with God. The gift of creation manifests this constitutive generosity of God: the angels are invited into the transparency of the Divine life. They enter into the depths of God, illuminated by the eternal Son and offered in the Spirit.

> The *Materiality* of their Kingdom was *spiritual*, and the Light that glanced through it, that filled its Transparency with an Infinity of glorious Wonders, was the Son of God, the brightness of the Father's Glory. The *Spirit* ... animated the inward Life of those glorious Angels, ... and moved with its sweet Breath, through all this *glassy Sea*, opening and changing new Scenes in the Mirror of Divine Wisdom.
>
> (*SP* 62)

Materiality is the medium of expression, of mutual knowing, the substance through which love passes and is received. This is why Law rejects the disjunction of body-machine and mind that he finds in the mechanical philosophy. It separates us from our "outwardness." Our fallenness may have deeply compromised our capacity to give ourselves in truth, but the mechanists have muted us in our very being. As for Law's unfallen angels, God's generosity does not limit them to being passive spectators. There can be no full sharing in the love of God that is not an active participation, in which God does not release and sustain the powers of the creatures that he loves. "All the *Powers* of Eternity, treasured up in their *glassy Sea*, unfolded themselves, and broke forth in ravishing Forms of Wonder and Delight, merely in Obedience to [the angels'] Call" (*SP* 8).

Commanding even the "Powers of Eternity," though, is both the height of their glory and the beginning of their fall.

They began to admire and even adore themselves, and to
fancy that there was *some Infinity of Power hidden* in themselves, which they supposed was kept under, and suppressed,
by that Meekness, and Subjection to God, under which they
acted. (*SP* 8)

The mythical drama moves onto its next and tragic phase.
The story of the angels that fell from heaven, thereby becoming
demons or devils, is at least as old as Christianity. The book of
1 Enoch, written during the second century BC, contains an early
version that influenced Christian writers. Here, though, the angels
fall through lust, seeking the "beautiful and comely daughters"
of the "children of men" (*1 Enoch* 6). The version that William
Law follows, in which the angels' sin is pride, became generally
accepted after the third century. Envious defiance and rebellion
against God drive Lucifer and his minions in the popular dramas of medieval England and in the most famous and elaborate
literary version, Milton's *Paradise Lost*.

The angels, then, or some of them, are baffled by their own
powers. They begin "to admire and adore themselves," slipping
into the illusion that "there was *some Infinity of Power hidden*
in themselves" (*SP* 6). Since all self-inflation is accompanied by
paranoia, in a heartbeat the angels jump from dreams of power to
conspiracy theory. God, they conclude, is keeping the true extent
of our abilities to himself:

With this proud Imagination, they boldly resolved, with all
their eternal Energy and Strength, to take their Kingdom,
with all its Glories, to themselves, by eternally abjuring all
Meekness and Submission to God. (*SP* 8)

"To take their Kingdom...to themselves." Law steers clear of
any anthropomorphic storming of heaven or suggestions of direct
violence taken against God. Milton, with some biblical warrant,

had avoided the absurdity by pitting Lucifer against the loyal angels.[3] Any battle imagery, though, would obscure Law's teaching about evil. Evil is self-destruction. The God of Jesus Christ, we remember, is not a wrathful God, so the fate of the angels is not externally imposed punishment meted out in anger. Nothing "cursed, or unhappy can be in, or come from God, but ... [the devils] have made that life which they must have in God, to be mere curse and unhappiness to them."[4] The angels make their own fate; they experience the truth of their own actions in the logic of their consequences. As a God who *manifests* himself, God tells, does, and allows truth. The angels "take their Kingdom ... to themselves, by eternally abjuring all Meekness and Submission to God" (*SP* 8). This is a declaration of independence, the seizure of a gift as if it were not and never had been a gift. The angels claim their own power to set up shop apart from God. The problem, of course, is that they do not have any power. They live in and by gift. This is no burden, no humiliation; the eternal persons of the Trinity themselves live in the mutual love of their self-giving. Seizing upon nothing, the angels are left with nothing except the burning agony of their desire. "Instead of Rising up above God (as they hoped) by breaking off from Him, there was no End of their eternal Sinking into new Depths of Slavery, under their own self-tormenting Natures" (*SP* 8).

In *The Way to Divine Knowledge* Law gives a slightly different version of the angelic fall. He shapes the story into a parallelism with the fall of Adam. Just as Adam fell through desire for knowledge of the creaturely world, looking below himself, the devil fell through desire for knowledge of the power of God, looking thus above himself. In both cases, though, a particular kind of knowledge is sought: instrumental knowledge, the means of control.

> The Angel turning his wandering Look into ... the *Might* and *Strength* of Eternity, that he might know *how* the

creaturely Life was *kindled* by it; and . . . so the Angel imagined to be like God, . . . [knowing] the Power of creating or kindling the creaturely Life. (*DK 58*)

The angels embroil themselves in a double contradiction. Not only do they seize as their own what they already enjoy as a gift, but also they try to pervert life, which exists only as a generous giving, into a commodity to be clutched, used, exploited. Again, the angels received according to the logic of their desire: they know the gift of life only in the form of their desire, as an enigma unilluminated by the love of God. They grasped "their own Nature, as they are in themselves, without God in them" (*DK 76*).

Law, following Boehme, adds a new theme to the classic myth by connecting the consequences of the angelic fall directly to the creation of our own world. He finds the biblical clue for this at the very beginning of Genesis:

And the earth was without form, and void; and darkness was upon the face of the deep. And the Spirit of God moved upon the face of the waters. (Gen. 1:2)

That glassy sea, the transparent, lively medium of angelic life and joy, turns into chaos, the void and formless waters. The angels' world, with themselves trapped within it, implodes as this roiling waste becomes the outward form of their furious and desperate desire. Clashing powers, forms sparking and consumed, panic, rage, and violent whirling — their glassy sea is pulled into "a horrible Chaos of Fire and Wrath, Thickness and Darkness, a Height and Depth of the confused, divided, fighting Properties of Nature" (*SP 6*). Apart from the mercy of God, who would not have such an ontological broil in his creation, this would have been "world without end." God's creative Word, however, the eternal Son, "stopped the Workings of these rebellious Spirits, by dividing the Ruins of their wasted Kingdom, into an Earth, a

Sun, Stars, and separated Elements" (*SP* 8). The rhythm of holy Wisdom ordaining "good out of evil to create" begins with the creation of the earth in which Adam is to rule.

For many Western Christians today, the fall of Lucifer has little positive theological charge for their faith and practice. With a theme that feels as alien as this, we tend to rush too quickly to the question "Do you believe this?" or, more generally, "You don't believe *this*, do you?" A little more caution is needed, so we must first ask what it all might mean. What is spoken of here that cannot be articulated as well or, perhaps, barely at all in other terms? In our context, that means enquiring as to the particular intimations of Law's version of the myth. The fallen angels contradict their own being, and their world becomes a welter of destruction, the chaos in which all form, all order is consumed: "So are they whirled down by the Impetuosity of their own wrong turned Wills, in a continual Descent from the Fountain of all Glory, into the bottomless Depths of their own dark, fiery, working Powers" (*SP* 8). We can take this as warning against a popular tendency to render the devil as a figure of Byronic sexiness, evil but personally rather alluring, even sympathetic. Law emphasizes the disintegrative chaos of evil, its "boundless, incessant, strong Rage, Darkness, and Strife" (*DK* 212). Should we think of the devil as a "person" at all? Law gives us little encouragement. He does, though, encourage us to think of personality in terms of communication, ultimately of that transparency to God and neighbor that we call love. Every choice of our own interests at the expense of others, every decision to isolate ourselves or to lie, deceive, and manipulate others as if they were things not persons, all the associate passions of "Covetousness, Envy, Pride, and Wrath" chip away at the personality, freeze it a little, turn us into the objects that we make of others. If evil originates in a spiritual choice, a self-separation from the light and love of God, then we best think of it as essentially antipersonal. Law evokes a collapse of the self, an appalling truncation of the creature, a frantic and disorderly will:

> Without or separate from the Light and Goodness of the Deity in them, [the fallen angels] are in themselves only the Thickness, and Rage, and Darkness, of an omnipotent *Compressing*, and omnipotent *Resistance* to it, and omnipotent *Whirling* from these two omnipotent Contrarieties.
>
> (*DK* 212)

In Scripture the light falls upon God and his ways, and the demonic does not appear independently of that focus. Jesus and his merciful power are in the foreground, not the demons that he casts out, which shriek and vanish into the night. The Bible does not authorize much interest in the devil, so we should be cautious in saying very much. If we are to say anything, though, it is better not to accord Satan the compliment of personality but rather to think of agency without light, will without reason, reckless hatred, and what Coleridge said of Shakespeare's Iago, "motiveless malignity."[5]

In Law's telling, the creation of this temporal world is God's act of faithfulness, faithfulness to his will to manifest himself in a particular history in which being is given and will not be taken back. This world is good brought out of evil, the order out of the chaos. The upshot of this is that the world is "very good" but not perfect. The world is not and never has been without danger, without a pull toward destruction, chaotic tendencies, entropy.

> The Disorders that were raised by *Lucifer* are not wholly removed, but Evil and Good must stand in Strife, till the last purifying Fire, here every Kind and Degree of Life,...is a Mixture of Good and Evil in its Birth. (*SP* 11)

The "mechanical philosophy" gave us a world that turned around humanity and instrumental reason, around modernity's promise of control. Our tendency to reduce evil entirely to sociological and psychological terms corresponds to this and suggests more pride than enlightenment. The myth of angelic fall may be baffling and barely imaginable, but it has the merit of response to biblical suggestions that evil cannot be accounted for in entirely anthropocentric terms.

God makes nothing evil, nor, however, Law tells us, does he make anything that is not, in some degree, in his image:

> God could not bring any creature into existence, but by deriving into it the self-existent, self-generating, self-moving qualities of his own nature: . . . and therefore, every creature must be finite, and must have a self-motion, and so must be capable of moving right and wrong, of uniting or dividing from what it will, or of falling from that state in which it ought to stand.[6]

Love refused is the fall at the origin of evil. This means that evil has to be told as a story, not explained by a theory. We cannot penetrate the will to evil, in the sense of reducing it to something other than freedom, and a freedom that always appalls us. Law himself goes a little too far when he speculates that inexperience lies at the root of the angel's fall. "No pure, intelligent, good, and holy created Being, can possibly lose this Divine State of Perfection, but through the first Use of its untried State and Powers" (*DK* 57). If we must avoid theoretical explanations of evil, we should also resist the temptation to defend God by relieving him of all responsibility. Again, Law goes too far when he says, "Here may be seen at once, in the clearest light, the true origin of all evil in the creation, *without the least imputation upon the creator.*"[7] In his infinite freedom, God creates a world in which evil can and will be a reality. The will to evil, whether angelic or human, God certainly wills as a free movement, but he does will it. To say anything less is to forget that God is *infinite* will and to suggest that he causes some things while leaving others to themselves. God is not justified by our explanations, however well meaning. God is justified by what he *does* in Jesus Christ, by the work of bringing good out of evil. At the fulfillment of all things, as Law knows, all tears will be dried, all pain assuaged, and only gratitude and praise remain.

An Address Named Paradise

And now we come to Adam. Law's portrayal of Adam is both suggestive and problematic; in some ways it is the weakest part of his later theology and the point at which appear the least fruitful aspects of his appropriation of Boehme. Adam enjoys a paradise of "*Peace* and *Unity* . . . a sweet Habitation of Divine Joy," yet this is also the site and substance of former chaos, an earth brought to fruition out of impossible strife.[8] However, God has wrested the warring, chaotic elements from the power of the fallen so that "they could kindle no more Wrath . . . anywhere but in themselves" (*DK* 215). Nevertheless, though this is now a peaceable kingdom, over which Adam is "Lord and Ruler," it is still a "mixture of heaven and hell" (*SP* 57). God's hand, and Adam's faithfulness, hold this peace, which, if broken, will turn the world back toward chaos. Law reminds us again that the Triune God brings his creatures into the working of the Divine life, a share in its joy and manifesting activity. Adam was "an heavenly artist, that had power and skill to open the wonders of God in every power of outward nature" (*SP* 7). We notice here that Law has appropriated a celebrated vocation of his own culture. Boyle and Newton also understood humanity's task in this way, and Abraham Cowley imagined scientific investigation as the way to God's promised land, celebrating the Royal Society as its conquerors:

> A better Troop she ne're together drew.
> Methinks, like Gideon's little Band,
> God with Design has pickt out you.

Although Law's spirituality is often regarded, with some justice, as "world-renouncing," he nevertheless envisions the human calling as inextricable from "Nature" — that is, from the human environment. In art, in makings and discoveries, humanity is to serve earth's revealing of Father, Son, and Spirit. After the fall, Law thinks, this calling is gravely limited and constrained but certainly does not disappear. This is clear not only in his, albeit qualified, appreciation of Newton and Freke, but also in the lives in *A Serious Call* of such as Miranda, whose charitable, restorative practices display God's mercy. Adam also inhabits his world as a peacekeeper — a detail of enormous significance, especially in relation to the sinister implications of modernity's harsher language urging the scientist to violate or torture Nature for the revelation of its secrets. No more than the angels in heaven, then, is Adam's role passive; he is "to do all that in this outward World, which God would have to be done in it before it could be restored to its first State" (*SP* 78).

As the "Lord and Ruler" of nature, Adam shares in the materiality of nature. Adam participates, therefore, in the substance of this earthly paradise, his body taken from the matter of chaos brought to God's good order. A "Body of this World" was the "*Medium* or *Means* through which he was to have Commerce" with this environment within which he was to do God's work as a "restoring angel." Since he lives in the world as master of the peace, the once warring elements have no power over Adam: "Neither Sun, nor Stars, nor Fire, nor Water, nor Earth, nor Stones, could act upon him, or hurt him." No surprises here, perhaps, but Law takes Adam's freedom from the dangers of materiality a troubling stage further. Adam is not simply spared the irritation of mosquito bites, the debilitations of disease, and the agonies of bruised and broken limbs; the world is unable to affect him in any way whatsoever, "to make any Impressions, or raise any Sensations in him" (*SP* 7). Adam's commerce with creation is thereby rendered entirely "one-way," a startling truncation of

Law's otherwise importance insistence on the unity of creatures and nature. His explanation of what this might be like is not reassuring:

> An Angel, we read, used at a certain Time to come down into a *Pool* at *Jerusalem;* the Water stirred by the Angel gave forth its Virtues, but the Angel felt no Impressions of *Weight*, or *Cold* from the Water. This is an Image of *Adam's* first Freedom from, and Power over all outward Nature. He could wherever he went, do as this Angel did, make every Element, and elementary Thing, discover all the Riches of God that were hidden in it, without feeling any Impressions of any kind from it. (*SP* 7)

Is there, though, no paradisal joy in tasting, smelling, in a surprising, unexpected sound, in running one's fingers along the back of the genial tiger? And, if not, what are we to say of our own bodily "sensations" as Adam's fallen heirs? May they never be enjoyed as God's merciful gifts without the dispiriting reminder that were we as we should be, we would not feel them at all? To be fair, at one point Law qualifies his claims by noting that Adam "neither saw nor felt either his own outward Body, or the Things of this outward World, *in the Manner, as we now see, and feel them.*"[9] Law does not expand on this, though, or follow it with any celebration of how Adam does feel the creation in and on his body. The weight falls on not feeling, on the indirection and distance of Adam's engagement with nature.

It is significant that seeing is implicitly exempted from the senses upon which the world makes no impression. In contrast with the "up close and personal" senses of touching, tasting, smelling, and even hearing to some degree, seeing is done at a distance. The word *spectator*, for instance, often carries the value judgment of "not engaged," "uncommitted," "not personally involved." Again, aspects of modern culture that Law elsewhere rejects creep in by a back door. Inscribed in Adam's bliss is the mechanistic alienation from nature: humanity is de-environmentalized and placed "above" nature, and nature is subordinated to the gaze of controlling, instrumental reason. Law's reading of Adam thus ends up pulling apart soul and body as surely as does the mechanical philosophy.

Closely connected with Adam's detachment from nature is Law's assertion that "he had no difference from an Angel in Heaven, but that this World was joined to him, and put under his Feet" (*SP* 78). Adam and his posterity are angels in temporary accommodation:

> *Adam* in his first Perfection, created by God to be a Lord and Ruler of this new-created World, to people it with an Host of angelic Men, till Time had finished its Course, and all things fitted to be restored to that State, from which they were fallen by the Revolt of Angels. (*SP* 78)

Those who are redeemed in Christ are also redeemed for this, to become as angels in heaven. This surely is a disappointing reading of both Adam and redemption. To put it bluntly, I do not particularly want to be an angel. I have spent far too much time busying myself in the flesh not to want it to count for something. That, as I understand it, is part of what is meant by the "resurrection of the body." Not, as Law seems to think, that we end up with the "bodies" of angels, but rather that the bodies we receive in resurrection are celebrations, honorings, of our earthly material history. They are unimaginably different and yet recognizable, recognizable as Jesus was recognizable frying Easter fish by the Sea of Galilee. I not only expect, I want to bear in eternity, material memories of the history that I have lived, just as Jesus bears the marks of nails. The angelic destiny that Law proposes is limited in another way, too: it does not do justice to his conviction that God's glory, the triumph of his love, is in bringing good out of evil.

> Oh my Friends, what a wonderful Procedure is there to be
> seen in the Divine Providence, turning all Evil . . . into a fur-
> ther Display and Opening of new Wonders of the Wisdom
> and Love of God! (*SP* 85)

That the materiality of the temporal world returns to nothing
and the breach in heaven's angelic ranks is closed is not victory
but rather repair. If the Triune God embarks on this difficult and
irrevocable history, the end must be more glorious than the beginning, must bring, surely, an unexpected and unprecedented
wonder out of all our woe. Only then is good truly brought out
of evil, only then is evil really put to work for good. This is what
Scripture teaches us to expect, the vision of Revelation hardly
being just a repetition of the paradise of Genesis.

Eve is notably absent from Law's discussion of Adam in Paradise. Only in *The Spirit of Prayer*, however, do we learn why.
Law has taken over from Boehme a more complex narrative of
the fall, according to which Eve is created only after Adam's desire
begins to slip from God toward the world. Adam was created androgynous, a perfect and harmonious unity of the qualities that
we identify as "masculine" and "feminine." In this original condition, Adam's heirs would be born "by the pure power of a Divine
Love" (*SP* 63). They would come to be, Law suggests, as all realities came to be, from the ideal forms of Eternal Nature. As God's
image, Adam was to engender his posterity out of his own participation in the Divine wisdom. A shadow, though, begins to come
over Adam's love for God as he begins to desire to create in his
own right, apart from his participation in the Divine image. His
first failure of love consists, then, in the refusal of a gift, the gift
of a sharing in God's creativity. God's response is to give again,
to come up behind Adam's withdrawal with another gift.

> The first Step therefore towards the Redemption or Recovery
> of Man, *beginning* to fall, was the taking his *Eve* out of him,
> that so he might have a *second Trial* in Paradise. (*SP* 85)

Since Adam now "stood with a longing Eye, looking towards the Life of this World" (*SP* 64), God gave that Adam might still have heirs and, in desiring Eve, still desire the original gift of God's love, albeit now in the separated form of his female counterpart.

Law insists, with some suspicious bluster, that one must be as spiritually thick as mud to miss the Bible's plain witness to Adam's androgynous condition. The exegesis, though, is spurious. He takes the idea from Boehme and justifies it with reference to a couple of passages from the early church fathers, and he clinches the case by appealing to a saying of Jesus: "In the resurrection they neither marry, nor are given in marriage, but are as the angels in heaven" (Matt. 22:30). And, he points out, if they are to be angels in the end, they must also have been in the beginning, in Adam. We are back with the same problem; Law turns away, in spite of his best instincts elsewhere, from our embodied particularity. Our future glory, he tells us, is "to be no more Male or Female, or a Part of the Humanity, but such perfect, complete, undivided Creatures, as the Angels of God are" (*SP* 60). It is hard to see, though, how an eschatologically "androgynized" me is still me. Heaven, no doubt, transforms all things, but not to the loss of ourselves, the earthly, gendered realities that God has accompanied so mercifully. An androgynous Adam, too, may be an image of completeness or wholeness, but is it really a Christian one? That Law thinks it is reflects his tendency to see the image of the Trinity in terms of the individual's interior dynamics rather than as the relations of persons. If God is a Triune life of love, then the unity of different persons in love, such as that of man and woman, is a rather better image of perfection than is the androgynous Adam. Thankfully, and to his credit, especially because the same cannot be said for Boehme, Law does not use Eve's lateness on the creative scene as an excuse for misogyny. Rather the reverse: Eve is the true bearer of hope; she is a greater gift than Adam knows, since "the Saviour of the World is called the *Seed of the Woman*, and had his Birth only from the female Part of our divided Nature" (*SP* 90).

Fallen Humanity

Why and how does Adam fall? Law must persuade against the intuitions of his time that more rationalizing theologies were already voicing. Why such terrible consequences for what is surely no more than a misdemeanor? What is more, eating from that tree was only a single infraction, one peccadillo. Is God that hard a taskmaster, more of a stickler than we would tolerate in a human being? This is more of that arbitrariness that Christians have foisted on God. From what we have seen already, we can anticipate Law's reply. He will try to show that eating the fruit symbolizes an interior change that is fundamental and momentous, that it turns upon the will not the deed. The consequences, he will argue, are the unfolding of the logic of that change, not an arbitrary punishment inflicted by an angry God. Above all, he will claim that from the very moment of catastrophe, God begins a counterprocess, a way for the prodigal out of the far country.

How can it happen at all? If Adam is the perfect creature of Law's description, what could prompt his utterly self-destructive withdrawal from the goodness of God? The idea of Adam going to ruin with open eyes is absurd. This

> intelligent Creature . . . cannot knowingly choose Misery, or the loss of its Happiness: Therefore it can only fall by *such* an Ignorance, or *Power* of falling as is consistent with its perfect State. (*DK* 54–55)

Law's direct answer to the problem is a good try but, unfortunately, doomed at the outset because he explains the origin of sin by way of a situation in which sin already exists — the horse has already bolted. Though gifted and blessed, Law argues, Adam was still vulnerable because he was inexperienced. Since experience can be gained only through experience, the initial weakness, whereby Adam had not fully gained possession of himself, so to speak, was "not a Defect, but a necessary Part of its first perfect State" (DK 55). Law has already made a similar point with reference to the angels, and now he applies the logic to Adam. An intelligent creature may attend to God or its attention may "wander." Our powers of attention, though, are strengthened by experience. So, "as a free, intelligent Creature, it could not be without this Power of thus turning its intelligent Eye; and yet, as a beginning Creature, that had no *Experience*, this Power could not be free from a *Possibility* of wandering" (DK 55). The more Adam enjoys the blessings of Paradise, therefore, the less vulnerable he is to any temptation that would draw his love away from God. Experience stabilizes his desire. The rationalist critic might retort, though, that if this is a "testing" of Adam, as Law describes it elsewhere, it is not a very fair one. Could not God sustain Adam through this period of experiential minority? Law would deny, though, that there was anything arbitrary about this "trial," since it was "not imposed upon him by the mere Will of God, or by Way of Experiment; but...necessarily implied in the Nature of his State" (SP 5). A more profound difficulty for Law is that if it takes time for Adam to settle into an unclouded desire for God, then his desire is not, at first, wholeheartedly set on God. If that is so, then something other than God is attractive to him, which simply means that he is *already* entangled in sin.

Law is so concerned to defend God from the charge of arbitrariness that he has succumbed to the rationalist itch himself and, as so often with scratching, only made things worse. He wants to render the sin of a "perfect" creature psychologically intelligible, not just this sin or that, but sin itself, that perverse curve of the heart that precedes all we do, think, and feel. He tries, therefore, to get behind our condition, imagining a perfection that, nevertheless, chooses sin. This, though, not only reads into the Genesis story much for which it gives no encouragement, but also implies that in imagination we can lift ourselves outside the structural condition of sin. That, however, we cannot do, precisely because we do not just do "bad stuff" — we *are* sinners. St. Paul's passionate outburst is more definitive in this regard than anything in Genesis:

> For we know that the law is spiritual: but I am carnal, sold under sin. For that which I do I allow not: for what I would, that do I not; but what I hate, that do I.... For I know that in me (that is, in my flesh) dwelleth no good thing: for to will is present with me; but how to perform that which is good I find not. (Rom. 7:14–18)

Since Law starts, admittedly following much of the Christian tradition, with the assumption of Adam's perfection, his urge to make the fall intelligible gets him into logical contortions. The Adam of Genesis, though, is a more modest creature than many accounts of Adam reflect. The second-century theologian Irenaeus took a different tack by suggesting that Adam was not created perfect but rather as capable of growth into a perfect obedience and reflection of God. Adam begins, then, with a certain vulnerability, a weakness that needs strengthening. Law's Adam does the same, but Law tries to make that circle square with Adam's "perfect state."

The Pauline insight, though, is also found in Law's exposition: "When the intelligent Creature turns from God to *Self* or Nature, he acts *unnaturally*" (*SL* 478). Sin is "unnatural," perverse, a contradiction of the human vocation. When we understand and accept that vocation, we find that indeed we do that which we would not. Ultimately, sin does not "make sense." Particular sinful acts may appear attractive, natural, understandable, but they do so in consequence of sin as a "power" that holds us, precedes us, and yet has our allegiance, our consent. As Law and the Christian tradition generally have understood it, the power sin has over us is *chosen* by us; it is not a matter of coercion or accident, nor is it fully reducible to weakness or vulnerability. Law's difficulties proceed from his picture of Adam's perfection, which is, in turn, part of his effort to show that responsibility for sin is ours and may in no way "be charged upon God."[10] As Irenaeus implies, though, an initial imperfection is not exclusive of our responsibility. Furthermore, as was said earlier, the attempt to account for sin "without the least imputation upon the creator"[11] is ill conceived. Nothing occurs save by the will of God. That does not mean that I do not freely choose particular actions or that sin is God's doing rather than mine. The context of all my willing, though, is the will of God that wills, among all other things, that this or that is accomplished *freely.* As Augustine puts it, "The Almighty works in the hearts of men even the movement of their [free] will, thereby to work through them whatever he himself chooses." The issue upon which everything turns is what God does with the evil that he allows, how he suffers it on the cross, and how, through it, he fulfills his creatures within the mutual love of the Trinity.

Indirectly, though, Law does suggest a more helpful answer to the question "How could Adam sin?" This is a reminder of something familiar, though hugely important, about the nature of sin. As we have seen a number of times, God creates so as to include others in his own Triune life. Law puts this well as God's desire that the

> universal, incomprehensible Goodness, Happiness, and Perfections of the Deity, might be possessed as Properties and Qualities of *an own Life* in creaturely finite Beings. (*SL* 478)

God lavishes himself so unstintingly that the giving of his life creates other, nondivine centers who receive his life and goodness as their *own* life and goodness. God creates, therefore, within the circulating love of the Trinity. With the Son, in whom we are created, and through the Spirit, we offer the Father his very own life, already made over to us as our own. Adam's — and our — calling, then, is to the form of an answer, that wholehearted response of which only those are capable who have a life of their own. Sin is the refusal of that circulating love. Incomprehensible though it is, sin comes along as a contradiction of our creation that is possible only because God gives his "Perfections . . . as Properties and Qualities of *an own Life*" (*SL* 478). God makes us his, but only as we are *our own* also, and so only as we may, unaccountably, refuse his gift.

When Law explains the character of Adam's sin, what it is that constitutes so momentous a self-perversion, his interpretation of Genesis seems rather feeble. The inexperienced Adam, before his love has properly settled into the love of God, begins to "cast a wandering Look into *that*, which he *was not*" and is so "*Reasoning* and Conjecturing about a certain *Good* and *Evil*, which were no Part of his own created State" (*DK* 55). The root of sin seems little more than curiosity, a rather intellectualist proposal generated partly because Genesis speaks of the "knowledge" of good and evil. What, in Law's view, is so sinister about wanting this knowledge? When Law looks out of his window, he sees a world in which crops fail, neighbors grow infirm, infants die in the trauma of birth, and if the lion does lie down with the lamb, you can be sure that only one of them is eating dinner. The world is in strife, violence abounds, life sets about life, competing, excluding, exploiting, killing. It is a world of good and evil, and Law, along with every sinner, knows it. According to Law's reading of Genesis, Adam wanted to experience the world like this. Put differently, Adam wanted to know the world *on his own terms*, and that meant, or turned out to mean, not knowing it as God's creation but rather seeing it as if, so to speak, God's hand were being removed, leaving Adam "in charge." Adam thus "finds Nature . . . as it is in *itself*, and *without* God" (*SL* 478).

Law's most searching exposition of Adam's sin is not in his discussion of Genesis but rather in a characterization of what he terms simply "Self." God's desire is to share his own love, wisdom, and happiness, his perfections, with finite creatures that possess them "as Properties and Qualities of *an own Life*." In God's intention, "Self" is the form in which we enjoy him. We are, therefore, created as "gift-receivers," our vocation being to live as dramas of gratitude. "All is a gift. He who receives the gift is himself the first gift he receives."[12] What happens, though, if we privilege ourselves over the God through whose generosity we are selves in the first place? As Law depicts him, Adam is really the first Deist: he does not want to be entirely "without God," but he does want God to remain at a respectful distance, to hand over the gift of creation but without the primary and continual gift of God himself. As one sixteenth-century theologian put it, "By pride we wish to rest in our own sphere, leaving divine things to God."[13] Adam was created to know the world "in God," a knowledge that comes to us once again, though differently, as we know the world "in Christ." The "knowledge of good and evil" is the experience or "sensibility," to use Law's term, of the world without the peace in which God knows, loves, and holds it. Disastrously, Adam turns "from God to *Self*" (*SL* 478). The "Self," though, is essentially a form of reception, a vessel for the Spirit. This is our glory and happiness, that we are made to contain God. However, closed in upon ourselves, referring life to the measure of ourselves, making ourselves the center, we can neither be satisfied by the world nor keep the peace. Inside and out, hell is awake.

Adam, of course, is us. What happens here happens everywhere, in everyone who bears a human face. The heart curves inward upon itself; we prefer ourselves, we work around ourselves, and we do not believe, not just on most days but never, that whosoever would find life must give it over. And though we have never known anything else, though there was no innocent moment, yet when God reaches us, we know that it was all according to our will. That the Adam and Eve story is set in the past, though, is still important. We are reminded of our inheritance, of a solidarity across all the unimaginable difference, with the first group of our ancestors who, in some long-forgotten form, heard God and, in the harsh misery of their lives, perhaps unsurprisingly, preferred themselves.

Law has already taught us the basic rhythm of God's ways. God committed his faithfulness in the choice to create. Grace surrounds chaos, preceding and following, and so the turn toward disaster is accompanied by a new movement of love. The significance of Eve is now revealed more fully: she is to bear the One who will restore and complete the great work, the *Mysterium Magnum*, as Boehme calls this tremendous labor of eternal love. Humankind, though, is not condemned to a long period of abandonment until this child finally shivers into the world in a Bethlehem outhouse. The Son, who then assumes flesh right to the fingertips, is also given to the wretched pair in Eden. He is the light or the "inspoken" word that stakes its place in the human heart and prepares the way of the Lord from the beginning, accompanying us every inch into the far country:

> A Beginning of a new Birth, called the *Seed of the Woman*, was, like the first Breath of Life, *breathed* or *inspoken* again into the Light of their Life, which, as an *Immanuel*, or *God with them*, should be born in all their Posterity, and be their Power of becoming again such Sons of God, as should fulfill the first Designs of the Creation of *Adam*. (*SP* 95)

And so the work continues. The form of Jesus is to be the form of all humanity, and so, whenever Jesus comes, whether "to his own" in Galilee (John 1:11), or in the witness of the church, he has laid his own ground beforehand, within us, "living, stirring, calling, knocking at the Door of thy Heart" (*SP* 27). We conclude this section, then, once more brought back to where everything begins: "From the Creation of *Adam*, through all the Degrees of his Fall to the Mystery of his Redemption, everything tells you, that God is Love" (*SP* 95).

The Return of the Prodigal

"Baby's on Fire"

"There was no End of their eternal Sinking" (*SP* 8). For the angels, there is no break between rebellion and the full weight of disaster. They and their world, built up in the joy of God, implode into chaos. With Adam and Eve it is different. Everything changes, they run and hide from God, which is the greatest change of all, and they grab whatever suits to cover the nakedness of which they are now ashamed. However, though the light dims into terrifying shadow, they are still standing. Why do Adam and Eve not go the way of Lucifer? What keeps them from complete destruction? Between the choice of self over God and the absolute anguished frustration brought by that choice stands the body. According to Law, the body, the particular form of our materiality, holds sin and destruction apart, although, frail and mortal, the body cannot keep this threatened peace for long:

> There was nothing that kept [Adam] out of the Hell of Fallen Angels, but his *Body* of Earthly Flesh and Blood, and as this was now as *mortal* in him, as it was in the Beasts . . . standing as it were on the Brinks of Hell, liable every Moment to be pushed into it. (*SP* 17)

Angels are spirit; they enjoy a heavenly materiality. Entirely subject and obedient to their wills, angelic bodies are the immediate music of their desire. When their love turns from God, at once all is discord and loss. Our bodies are not like that; they have

139

their own way, acting alongside and even upon our thoughts and intentions. Their rhythms exceed our knowing, their demands resist our wills, their whirrs and rumbles proceed from a million engagements and exchanges beneath our awareness: growing, changing, defending, breaking down, sustaining. Our bodies unite us with ourselves and connect us with others. They also divide us. As our bodies have their own ways, we cannot simply have our way with them, and they separate us from others, whom we know only through the material world that we share, through sensory touch and the public web of language. Since we are embodied, we have our being in materiality and thus within a material world through which we are to hear, find, and make trial of the love of God. Our bodies give us time, a stake in change, an arc of movement and possibility. They are the parcel of flesh and blood that we know best, and yet a mirror takes us by surprise, while ecstasy makes the body strange, and pain makes it feel like an enemy. The body's persistent strangeness — its need for care, its resistance to our wills — is both an image and a vehicle of our vocation. We must hear the God who comes as a stranger, as a word alien to our fallen selves, and who, through our materiality, makes the way to a lasting peace.

By interpreting our earthly materiality as the "buffer" between sin and destruction, Law takes the body up into that binding theological motif according to which God is always in advance of evil, as soon as it appears, putting it to work for a greater, if mysterious, good. Elsewhere, though, Law describes the body in more unsettling terms. Having inflated the perfections of Adam to an unnecessary extreme, he then reacts upon fallen humanity with a vengeance. We are trapped beneath a sickly "covering" of flesh, burdened by a "dark, gross, heavy, fleshly Body."[1] Yes, indeed, fallen men and women are subject "to Heat and Cold, to Pains and Sickness, Horror of Mind, disturbed Passions, Misery, and Fears of Death" (*SP* 12). In an extra twist, though, the body becomes one-sidedly the vehicle of ill, condemned as "Death and

Darkness," naturally corrupt, "impure, bestial Flesh and Blood." This strays too far toward occluding the persisting goodness of creation. That abiding goodness, which makes the body itself a cry for mercy, is a form of the faithfulness of the God who lets his sun and rain fall on bad and good alike (Matt. 5:45). By and large, Law follows the Pauline use of "flesh" to refer to our condition "as [it] is by the Fall," but still there is that telltale slip by which condemnation gravitates to the body itself, as "gross," "impure," flesh and blood. We might blame this on Boehme, who occasionally lets himself go with some graphically nasty remarks on the body, but Law was writing harshly about the body in *A Serious Call*, having Eusebia describe it as "infected clothes that fill you with ill diseases and distempers which oppress the soul with sickly appetites and vain cravings" (*SC* 270). There is a line from Law's nervous rejection of "idle pleasures" and "leisure" to the angelic Adam untouched by any sensations arising from creation around him. Law fails to develop the motif of the body as a merciful barrier to chaos into a theology of the body as blessing. He understands the gospel as God's declaration of peace and the fallen state as characterized by violence, a field of unquenchable conflict. His one-sided account of bodiliness, however, risks encouraging a repressive, oppositional relationship to the body and all that proceeds from it. Thereby spiritual practice itself becomes all too invested in violence.

Inside and outside, Adam's world is of a piece:

> Paradise being departed from the Earth (which before kept all in harmony) now Discord and Contrariety broke forth in *all* the Elements, and Animals upon it....From this time *Storms* and *Tempests*, *Thunders* and *Lightnings*, *Earthquakes*, and all sorts of Strife and Contrarieties through all temporal Nature; and in *Man*, and other *Animals*, arose the same *Disquiet*; for the Elements *in* and *without* man, were of the same Nature.[2]

For us, this is another of those especially alien elements in the myth. The age of the universe, the latecoming of human life on earth, the plenitude of nonhuman life, and the intricacy of ecological dependence make us recoil from the claim that Adam's fall was felt "through all temporal Nature." Absorbing the "evils" of the nonhuman nature so entirely into the terms of human sinfulness seems implausibly, if not dangerously, anthropocentric. Before we discard it, though, we should attend carefully to this moment in the story. "Very good" though God judges it, this world is not yet the fullness of creation. Christians recognize that even Nature groans and strains against the prodigality of its losses and destructiveness, against all the apparently purposeless, wasteful suffering. All life tends, like a question, toward that "new heaven and earth" promised through the seer of the book of Revelation. Christian hope is for all creation. As to the connection between sin and the nonhuman world, Law's declaration that now "the *Elementary* Nature *in* Man, and Beasts, was in the *same* Disorder with the *outward* Elements and Stars" is today gaining a peculiarly uncomfortable point. The more humanized the world becomes, the more the nonhuman world is incorporated within human cultural and technological systems, the more it is rent, disturbed, and threatened by human violence. This is not a condemnation of the process as such; human beings have been turning nature into culture from the moment someone noticed that sharp stones might chop trees or split heads. Technology is our way, indeed, part of our calling. Law's Adam, we noticed, is not supposed to leave things alone. The consequences, though, of the fateful entwining of our energies and passions with creation remind us how far the process is from innocence and what is at stake in it. This theological story in which human sin provokes natural ruin is, perhaps, best read as prophecy.

"Discord and Contrariety broke forth in *all* the Elements, and Animals upon [Earth]." The root of this maelstrom is frustrated love. Since God is love, the unqualified will to goodness, every-thing that God does is done in love and for love. Looking along the line opened up by Law's faithfulness to Trinitarian theology, we recognize the mutual love of Father, Son, and Spirit as their eternal giving and receiving of themselves from one another. Cre-ating, as Law suggests, is the mobilization of this love in finite forms of receiving and giving. Creation is the making of "lovers." As Law has reminded us several times, this is entirely a matter of gift and not a "one-off" gift. To be created is to exist through and in the continuous giving of God. Creation is only active in good-ness, from the tiniest creature finding its ecological place, to the sacrifices of human care, insofar as it exists as a receiver of good-ness. First and foremost, then, creation is a form of reception, a need for the goodness that it receives. Since nothing that God does is done except as an exchange of love, everything that he gives fulfills the creatures to whom he gives it, in everything God is their one desire. "The young lions roar after their prey, and seek their meat from God" (Ps. 104:21). We should remember *Christian Perfection* here. Law's thesis is that "perfection" is not a special goal, a vocational extra, over and above an ordinary life and only for the religiously "special." Law can argue this because he grasps Christian perfection as the fulfillment of humanity and the earthly anticipation of heaven. If this is true, then the loving action, the grace that works this perfection in us, cannot be an "extra" to human happiness, the spiritual cherry on an otherwise entirely satisfactory cake. God does not give gifts like that: God is always essential. We may resist the vocation to perfection, but insofar as we do, we are odds with ourselves because we exist as the desire for this perfection: that is what we *are*. It follows that if there is "Discord and Contrariety," then the loving desire that we are as creatures has been frustrated, or, more accurately, in turning from God, we have turned against, frustrated ourselves.

In itself, "Nature" is only "a Want and Hungering" (*DK* 83). God did not design his creation to be self-satisfied; on the contrary, he made it as a longing for himself and nothing less than himself. For the sake of this point, Law quarrels both with Deists and with the easygoing preachers of cheap grace. Both urged what modern Christianity has so often and tragically become: a religion for immanent satisfactions, with God merely waiting quietly on the eschatological sideline, ready to dispense immortality when finally needed. God, though, made creatures through love, from his eternal desire, and he made them to exist as desire for that love. Desire is the key to Nature: "Every Thing had its Beginning in it, and from it; and every Thing is led by it to all its Happiness" (*DK* 236).

There is, though, "desire" and "desire." When we lack, we long until our need is met. We must distinguish, though, between the desire that proceeds from want and the desire that, as it is continually satisfied, only expands the more to receive. The latter is love consummated as only God can; it is the life of heaven. Those whose

> desire is fulfilled, rejoice in possessing God; they never cease to have their desires satisfied, and are never the least wearied, and being unwearied, they never cease to desire.[3]

Compared with this vision, how stingy and mean-spirited is our conventional hope that our loved ones should "rest in peace"; how carelessly it sells out "peace." The peace of heaven is more active, more energetic, mobile and sprightly than we can possibly imagine. We do not "rest." Rest is just the terminus of desire, an end to the aching of want. Heaven is desire transformed from the longing of fallen nature to the insatiable satisfaction of love. Until then, though,

> the Working of Nature must be in Want, in Pain, and Dis-satisfaction, till God (the Blessing and Fulfilling of Nature) is manifested, found, and enjoyed in it. (*DK* 197)

Law's analysis of the violence that this "Want, Pain, and Dissatisfaction" necessarily involve draws on Boehme's teaching of the "seven properties" of Nature. To some extent, this is overkill, as Law makes only a selective use of this scheme and too much is left unclear. In particular, though, there are some intriguing hints; he never expounds the last four properties satisfactorily or deploys them so that they inform his treatment elsewhere of "new birth" and its consequences. Our exposition, therefore, can stay with the first three properties. These are Law's primary interest, and here his exposition is memorable and opens our way to understanding the work of Christ and the necessary "regeneration" that Christ achieves in us.

As Law interprets Boehme's scheme, the "first three properties" of Nature may be understood as answering this question: "If Nature is a longing desire for God, then what becomes of Nature should that longing desire no longer be satisfied?" To the extent that Nature turns away from God's light, love, and joy, Nature is riven by the contrary dynamics of unsatisfied desire. Losing its true object, desire turns in upon itself, dividing into two opposing forces or "properties." One force is centripetal, a "compressing" movement inward; the other is centrifugal, a drive outward, connecting with and "attracting" what is beyond. The fierce and irreconcilable opposition of these powers, the one a "Shutting up," the other a "Running out," turns them helplessly around one another, producing the third property: natural life as a "whirling Anguish."

> Now from this great and equally strong Contrariety of the *two first Properties* of the Desire, magically pulling, as I may say, two contrary Ways, there arises as a necessary Birth from both of them, a *third Property*, which is emphatically called a *Wheel* or *whirling Anguish* of Life. (*SL* 374)

The torment of these first three properties we have met before as the final condition of the fallen angels. After Adam's fall, though, the chaos of their ruin leaks back into creation, though still restrained by God's mercy. The oppositions and collisions of the three properties, the unconscious drives of Nature, are the spiritual reality rendered misleadingly predictable as mechanism in Newton's laws of motion. Despite the regularities celebrated by the mechanists, there is throughout Nature, according to Law, a frustrating, a crossing of life, an inner drift into conflict that St. Paul refers to as subjection to vanity:

> The earnest expectation of the creature waiteth for the manifestation of the sons of God. For the creature was made subject to vanity, not willingly, but by reason of him who hath subjected the same in hope, because the creature itself also shall be delivered from the bondage of corruption into the glorious liberty of the children of God. For we know that the whole creation groaneth and travaileth in pain together until now. (Rom. 8:19–22)

As regards ourselves, the "first three properties" are a vivid metaphor for a structural disturbance in the flow of human desire. Only the inexhaustible God can satisfy the insatiable drive of our desire. Sin, as we have seen, seeks satisfaction in an illusory independence from God. Under the governance of sin, therefore, desire takes charge of its own blessedness, constructing substitutes for God. In such an impossible condition desire divides against itself.

Our primary movement of self-love, through which we secure and maintain our own integrity, also demands connection with others, that we fit within an environment, drawing it around ourselves, giving ourselves to it. This necessary force impelling relationship, though, also threatens us with self-loss, capture, exhaustion, disappointment, the counterdesires of others. So, Law suggests, when human desire is deprived of its true, divine object, self-love turns violent, coming into conflict with the drive for connection: "The *one only* Will of the Desire... is to have That which it has not; and all it can do toward *having* it is to act as if it were *seizing* it" (*SL* 374). Desire oscillates in fearful anguish between a self-protection that stifles and isolates, subordinating others to itself, and a relating in which identity is lost and the self caught up in self-laceration, resentment, the perverse violence of the "weak." Despite the abstract presentation, we have not left those familiarly modern characters in *A Serious Call.* Law's admonitory characters are marked by inward conflict and the unstable investments of desire that deform their personality and relationships. Flatus is "always uneasy, and always searching after happiness," tumbling from one pastime to another, routinely disappointed. He seizes the next promise of joy, investing his desire in defiance of the emptiness that his passions never fill. So, Flatus swings from the peevishness of a frustrated self-love to the joyful embrace of another and equally doomed obsession. Then, there is the narcissistic Flavia, staking her soul on show, on relations as thin as veneer. Everything is controlled, not a pimple is left to chance, yet Flavia is still perpetually anxious, always at the mercy of her brittle relationships, the only ones that feel safe to form. Worse still is Matilda, who sacrifices her daughter's life to the cause of attracting a husband. Since Matilda is convinced that security lies only in beauty, the "second property" that connects, draws, and attracts overwhelms her child, who dies of beauty's discipline, "her ribs [having] grown into her liver" (*SC* 164–68 [Flatus], 105–9 [Flavia], 263–65 [Matilda]).

The modernity of Law's characters, their relative familiarity for us, is important. All theology bears the form of its time and culture, even when it is sharply critical and tears against it. Law's exposition of sin is no exception and reflects the modern world that was developing so fast during his lifetime. We may read it, therefore, both in the context of the long history of Christian teaching on sin and as a piece of specific cultural critique. In interpreting the contrarieties of fallen desire, Law discovers an abiding violence: a conflict between the self preserving and securing itself (the first property) and the self relating to, receiving from, and giving to its environment (the second property). To put it differently, individuality and sociality are at odds; society is necessary to self-preservation, but it is also threatening and embroils the self in an ongoing violence. Though this account of fallenness has precedents in older theologians, it is striking that a similar conflict between individual and society is the basis of some of the most influential and formative social philosophies of early modernity.[4] These accounts have decisively shaped modern notions of social and political life and continue to inform our anxieties, expectations, and hopes. Probably the most notorious of these, largely because of its materialist, if not explicitly atheistic, proposals, was Thomas Hobbes's *Leviathan*. Hobbes argues that self-preservation is the fundamental "right of nature," and that given the conflicts that arise from scarce resources, the natural condition of human beings is a state of war that serves to make human life "solitary, poore, nasty, brutish, and short."[5]

> *Out Of Civil States, There Is Alwayes Warre Of Every One Against Every One....* During the time men live without a common Power to keep them all in awe, they are in that condition which is called Warre; and such a warre, as is of every man, against every man.[6]

This perpetual war devours all unless human beings agree to the condition of society. Society involves them mutually agreeing to limits upon individual liberty and transferring to a ruling power the right to exercise coercion to keep the peace of this limited liberty. Violence is the natural condition of humanity. Nature sets us up for violence, and society restrains that violence but does so by violent means.

Back in 1723, three years before *Christian Perfection*, while still tutoring in Putney, Law composed a vigorous response to a witty but cynical account of society and the individual by Bernard

Mandeville. In *The Fable of the Bees or Private Vices, Public Benefits*, Mandeville agrees with Hobbes that human relationships are essentially aggressive and competitive. He understands that society is a necessary means of restraining unbridled competition but also of making the best of our aggressive proclivities. The latter is what particularly interests him. Mandeville's thesis is brutally simple: a prosperous society, indeed, any large society at all, needs vice like a fish needs water. If we desire a society comfortable enough to be worth living in, we are far better investing in greed, envy, unscrupulous competition, manipulation, dishonesty, and lying than in probity, truthfulness, charity, and fairness. In the doggerel of the fable itself, "all Trades and Places knew some Cheat; No Calling was without Deceit"; so, "every Part was full of Vice, / Yet the whole Mass a Paradise."[7] On the other hand, an easy situation, on some abundant island in which men and women live honestly, may be peaceable, but it is also boring.

> They shall have no Arts or Sciences...they must be poor, ignorant, and almost wholly destitute of what we call the Comforts of Life, and all the Cardinal Virtues together won't so much as procure a tolerable Coat or a Porridge Pot among 'em.[8]

The paradox that Mandeville wants us to accept is that although fierce strife and dishonesty are ubiquitous at the level of individual relations, the consequence for society as a whole is productivity, prosperity, growth, scientific advance, and artistic flourishing. Mandeville might have felt vindicated by Gordon Gekko's speech in the 1987 film *Wall Street*:

> The point is, ladies and gentleman, that greed — for lack of a better word — is good. Greed is right. Greed works. Greed clarifies, cuts through, and captures the essence of the evolutionary spirit. Greed, in all of its forms — greed for life, for

money, for love, knowledge — has marked the upward surge
of mankind. And greed ... will not only save Teldar Paper,
but that other malfunctioning corporation called the USA.

Moral virtue, though widely regarded, is socially effective only to
limit extreme misbehavior; in larger doses it undermines prosperity and general happiness. Besides, virtue itself, according
to Mandeville, is only a form of pride, a self-restraint inspired
by ideologies that preach it up as a mark of class superiority.
With a cynicism that drew a fury of counterarguments from
Law, Mandeville concludes that "Moral Virtues are the political
Offspring which Flattery begot upon Pride."[9]

Law finds Mandeville's argument appalling. Aside from in-
coherencies and exaggeration, Mandeville has done the dirty on
humanity. He touts sophisticated realism, but behind the superior
tone of worldly wisdom there is a cynical rejection of Christian
teaching. Mandeville refuses any engagement with that "Declaration of the Dignity of Man's Nature," according to which God
said, "Let us make man in our own image, after our likeness"
(Gen. 1:26).[10] Without comment, the secular horizon replaces the
theological. Introducing the section "An Enquiry into the Origin
of Moral Virtue," Mandeville tries to evade theological critique
by stating that he is writing "neither of Jews nor Christians, but
Man in his State of Nature and Ignorance of the true Deity."[11]
Law jumps on the disingenuity of this claim:

> The Observations, which you have made upon human Na-
> ture, on which your Origin of Moral Virtue is founded, are
> only so many Observations upon the Manners of *all Orders*
> of *Christians*.[12]

Throughout his treatise, Mandeville is describing the prosperous
society of the British and no less so when he imagines the process by which "virtue" was established among humanity. The
reconstruction of origins, though, is important to Mandeville as

it was to other secularizing social theorists. By arguing the shape of our social beginnings, philosophers projected their emerging capitalist society back into a mythicized historical past, full of secular Adams. Thus they endowed it with the force of ages or even nature itself.

Mandeville does not argue that sin constitutes the violence and competition of which society makes such agreeable employment. Aggressive competition and the vicious passions are a necessity of human relations, raised to good purpose in prosperous societies. Many such arguments reflected and reinforced early capitalism, its legislation, class relations, social discourse, politics, and economic practices. Thus political philosophies argued the theory behind a general conviction among Britain's old and newly wealthy that a government's primary duty was the protection of private property. The context for Law's teaching on sin is a society in which the "man of property" had become the paradigm individual, the human face of Britain. Society, in turn, is the field of competition from which his substance derives and by which it is threatened. The poor, the laboring classes, the products of whose work are so illiberally distributed, the interference of government, and the critical ideals of Christian faith all raise, in various ways, the threat of crimes against property. As such, the dangers that they pose must be resisted, if possible, eliminated. Law's reading of sin is important because, unlike Mandeville or Hobbes, he does interpret the conflict between individual liberty and social order as an expression of sin. The violence, the "private vices" that make social relations serve our striving for self-preservation, betrays our estrangement from God, the loss of our one true desire. From this perspective, Christian faith should challenge the naturalization, the "inevitability" of social violence. If such is the dynamic of sin, then without any illusions as to its persistence until the judgment, we must also insist, in the name of Christ, that grace disrupts this established disorder. The Spirit works the form of Christ in disconcerting exceptions to brutal normality. As Law writes to the clergy,

> The Gospel State could not be God's *last Dispensation*, or the finishing of Man's Redemption, unless . . . it brought *the Thing itself* . . . into *real Enjoyment*, so as to be possessed by Man in Spirit, and in Truth.[13]

The neediness of individuals, from which both Hobbes and Mandeville diagnose the necessity of violence, may itself be read otherwise. Catherine of Sienna, for instance, whose *Dialogues* Law would have read, insists that our experience of lack gives us "reason — necessity in fact — to practice mutual charity." God, therefore, says, "In this mortal life, as long as you are pilgrims, I have bound you with the chain of charity. Whether you want it or not, you are so bound."[14] Humanity's true horizon, however obscured by sin, is not the deadly dynamics of divided desire but rather the mutual giving of the Trinitarian persons, who are in their giving to one another. Our way is formed in Christ, who, emptying himself as the servant of all, received the "Name above all names" (Phil. 2:9). Only God, of course, can be the object of such complete self-giving; upon anything less, our insatiable desire divides into violent contraries.

The Word Within and Without

As we have followed it so far, Law's analysis of our fallen plight is one-sided. The one element that truly makes all the difference is still missing. For the full picture, we must return to the narrative as it opens up toward its goal in Christ:

> And no sooner had God informed this miserable Pair of the State they had brought upon themselves, but, in that Moment, his eternal Love *begins a Covenant* of Redemption,

that was to begin in them, and in and through them extend
itself to all their Posterity. (*SP* 95)

The "Covenant of Redemption" begins in the gift of the eternal Son himself, not yet in the full glory of his humility as the
incarnate Christ but rather as a word "inspoken" to the heart,

> like the first Breath of Life...an *Immanuel*, or *God with
> them*, [that] should be born in all their Posterity, and be
> their Power of becoming again such Sons of God. (*SP* 95)

The giving of the "inspoken Word" or "seed of Christ" is another
moment in the story of salvation whereby God turns disaster
into the beginnings of a greater good. Demonic chaos becomes
the Paradise of Adam, from Eve will come the "bruiser of the
serpent," and fallen humanity receives the word of Christ. Law
seizes on the motif of the "inspoken Word" to express three features of salvation that he considers crucial. In each case, he has in
mind positions that he considers false theological paths. Against
a Calvinist doctrine of predestination that narrows the company
of the elect to a few, the "seed of Christ" begins a process of
redemption that is universal in time and space.[15] "See here the
Beginning and glorious Extent of the *Catholic Church* of Christ,
it takes in all the World. It is God's unlimited, universal Mercy
to all Mankind" (*SP* 27). Against his usual suspects, the Deists,
Arians, and Socinians, all of whom relativize or reduce the significance of Jesus, this new beginning in grace reveals that "the
Holy Jesus" is nothing less than the origin and goal of redemption. Only the "whole process of Jesus Christ," from inspoken to
incarnate Word, "could *begin, carry* on, and *totally* effect Man's
Deliverance from the Evil of his own fallen Nature" (*SL* 444–
45). Finally, against modern Pelagians, who ascribe salvation, at
least in part, to human energies, this unmerited seed of Christ,
in Law's teaching, is the energy of divine life, "the working Will,
that bringeth forth the New Birth of Heaven in us"; so, this is

"from the Beginning to the End, the pure Grace of God to us, and no Salvation of our own" (*DK* 158).

Law uses the doctrine of the "inspoken word," therefore, to affirm that salvation is universally offered, that it is wholly the work of God, and that Jesus is its beginning, goal, and form. The doctrine, though, has some risks. Not without some embarrassment, Law discovered that his later works were popular among Quakers. Much of the attraction was that Law taught that a "seed of Christ" was given to all humanity, and that salvation consisted in its growth within the soul. The resemblances to Quaker doctrines of the "inner light" were striking. The problem was that Quakers appealed to the "inner light" in defense of their rejection of sacraments. This teaching had also fostered among Quakers a weakening of the classical Christian emphasis on God's "mighty works" for Israel and, supremely, in the incarnation. "Christ in us" was thus privileged over "Christ for us" — that is, in the life, death, and resurrection of Jesus. Were Law's Quaker readers onto something? Classically, Christians have confessed in these matters a definite "economy" or ordering. The work of God in Israel and in Jesus comes first, and from this follows the giving of the Spirit for the creation of the church as the body of Christ. The "regeneration" of men and women occurs through their participation in the church, its preaching, and its sacraments. Is, then, Law's doctrine of the "inspoken word," the work of Christ within us, part of a profound shift in Christianity's center of gravity? If so, then, as the weight falls increasingly on the inward change of individuals, the "mighty works" of God, all the way to Easter and Pentecost, begin to lose their substance, becoming illustrative or symbolic of "religious experience" and its behavioral consequences. Do Law's writings give us grounds to regard him as a would-be Quaker, just a little too shy perhaps to cast off his sacramental bathing trunks for a plunge into the sea of inwardness and silence?

Israel does not feature much in Law's later teaching.[16] His story moves, almost without a pause, from Adam to Christ. If his theology is retreating from history, this would be an obvious way to start, and if the material hurly-burly of Israel evaporates, then can Jesus of Nazareth, flesh and bone of Israel, preaching Israel's hope to Jewish crowds and nailed up by Roman soldiers, be far behind? Reading Law this way, though, goes against much that he does say. Israel's story is worryingly truncated, but the "inspoken Word" does not eliminate the Old Testament witness; rather, it is the condition for our hearing it as God intended:

> The *Faith* of the first *Patriarchs* could not have been in Being; *Moses* and the *Prophets* had come in vain, had not the Christ of God lain in a *State of Hiddenness* in every Son of Man.
>
> (*SL* 405)

Furthermore, the word of Moses and the prophets is precisely the annunciation of Jesus. This "hidden" Christ readies the soul to hear the witness to the visible Christ. The orientation of Law's doctrine, therefore, is toward "that Blessed Christ, that was born of the *Virgin Mary*" (*SP* 23).

Law's teaching on the body as the spirit's necessary outward form and his refusal to countenance any mechanistic distinction between spiritual mind and body-machine also provides a secure place for the sacraments.

> We must eat Christ's flesh, and drink his blood in the same reality, as he took upon him the real flesh and blood of the blessed virgin: we can have no real relation to Christ, can be no true members of his mystical body, but by being real partakers of that same kind of flesh and blood, which was truly his...that through him, the same might be brought forth in us.[17]

Finally, Law explicitly and stridently denies that an acceptance of the indwelling Christ implies any reduction in the importance of the Jesus of the Gospels:

> Let no one here think to charge me with Disregard to the
> Holy Jesus, who was born of the *Virgin Mary*, or with setting
> up an *inward* Saviour in Opposition to the outward *Christ*,
> whose History is recorded in the Gospel. . . . [I] will assert no
> inward Redemption but what wholly proceeds from, and is
> effected by that Life-giving Redeemer, who died on the Cross
> for our Redemption. (*SP* 23)

Of course, one may say that he "doth protest too much" and not
take him at his word. However, to do his work justice, we should
press the question that his denial begs. Does he succeed in giving an account of incarnation and atonement that hangs together
with this emphasis on "Christ within" yet in which "the outward
Christ" retains his place as the source of inward regeneration?

Despite the timeless and placeless character of Law's dialogues, contemporary urgencies inform the shape of his theology.
Foremost among his theological passions was the renewal of a
Christianity that brought and demanded substantial change. His
indignation at nominal Christianity and at what he saw as clerical
interest in preaching cheap grace is never far away. Christianity
must make us different, it must be the power of God making us
different, or it is nothing at all. That, together with an equally
uncompromising and controversial instance on the universality
of Christ's saving work, does much to explain Law's stress on
the "inspoken Word." A comparative tally of pages, therefore,
devoted to the "inward" and the "outward" Christ is no way
to decide their relative theological importance. Law consistently
identifies the "inspoken Word" with Jesus. The inward Christ
conforms our lives to the Jesus of the Gospels, and it is that
Jesus who must be recognized in them: "The boundless Humility and Resignation of the Holy Jesus; the unwearied Patience,
the unalterable Meekness, the impartial, universal Love of God,
manifested in my Soul; are [the] only Proofs, that God is in me of
a Truth" (*SP* 141). Jesus comes to us in the fleshly definition of

his history, showing us the marks of crucifixion, and he rises up within us, as we recognize the One for whom men and women have longed since Adam. Jesus is what history is about. There is no inner/outer opposition here, Law argues, anymore than when we say that a plant "has no Benefit from the Sun, till the Sun is thus *inwardly* forming, generating, quickening, and raising up a Life of the Sun's Virtues" (*SP* 23).

Perhaps, had Law allowed his Trinitarian intuitions greater play here, he might have made more of the relationship between Christ and the Spirit. He touches on this but leaves the two uncomfortably side by side: "Where the *Word*, or *Son* of God is, there is the Spirit of God in the *same State;* if one is only a *Seed* of Life, a Spark of Heaven, the other is so also; and these two, thus considered, are the glorious *Pearl* of Eternity, hidden in every Man's Soul" (*SP* 139). If Law had interpreted the "seed" given to Adam pneumatologically — that is, in terms of the Holy Spirit — that outward, connective movement of the Spirit, which we have mentioned before, would have guarded against the suggestion that the "ordering" of salvation was shifting its center of gravity away from God's self-giving in the outward flesh of history. The Spirit, after all, is precisely the Spirit of Jesus, the One who makes Jesus known, and through whom the light of Christ illumines us. The goal of the Spirit, who inspires the prophets as well as parting Red Sea waves, is Jesus, whose flesh the Spirit stitches in the womb, who receives the Spirit at his baptism, who offers the Spirit up in death, and who is raised by the Spirit. Law moves precisely in this direction in *The Spirit of Prayer*. "By the *Spirit* is meant the *Bruiser of the Serpent*, that Seed of the Light and Spirit of God, which lieth as a Treasure hid in the Soul." The Spirit brings us to the new birth, in which "the Nature, Spirit, and Tempers of *Jesus Christ* are opened in our Souls." The Spirit thereby forms not itself but rather always Christ, working in us the life of Jesus that "strengthened with might by his Spirit in the inner man ... Christ may dwell in [our] hearts by faith" (Eph.

3:16–17). Now, when we consider the full depth of our need for this "strengthening," we may see Law's way to "Christ without us," incarnate and crucified, as the necessary ground of "Christ within us."

If the Spirit works to form Christ in us, why is my Christian life so half-baked? Why do I persist in attitudes, actions, reactions, and habits such that, when I allow myself to catch up with myself, I know that I fall way short of my calling? From the first few pages, readers of A Serious Call had met with Law's answer to this. I am a sorry spectacle because I do not really want to be otherwise, I do not "intend to please God in all the actions of [my] life" (SC 56). Given a true intention, everything would be different: "Now, who that wants this general sincere intention, can be reckoned a Christian? And yet if it was among Christians, it would change the whole face of the world" (SC 58). Statements such as this provoked Wesley and the evangelicals. Law's Christianity seemed a burdensome promulgation of rigorous demand without the gracious means. I argued earlier that such a reading is superficial. Certainly, in his later works Law never gave up his claims about intention. After all, he found them in Jesus' own teaching: "A good man out of the good treasure of the *heart* bringeth forth good things" (Luke 6:45). No merely external observances, no dutiful routines in themselves, no intellectual acceptance of doctrines or historical "facts" are enough; what is needed is what Law, in the later writings, calls a "working will," by which our outward life becomes an expression of that on which the heart feasts. The rub, though, is that our willing is divided and contrary. When Adam fell, he lost wholeheartedness. Instead of that single desire, that fixed intention, that rests upon God and takes up all creation in loving God, we have ambiguous loyalties, misplaced hopes, a striving for life, even for good, that curves fatally toward the self. "What I would, that do I not; but what I hate, that do I" (Rom. 7:15). We desire anything but God, and yet our desire for God persists; it is what we are *for*. A creature whose vocation for God is written into its being, fallen men and women in whom the "inspoken Word" dwells, cannot love wholeheartedly any reality other than God. When they try, their own souls murmur against them. Integrity of desire, though, is the "heavenly life" that Adam lost and is beyond our reach. We cannot give and receive wholeheartedly, so far forget ourselves to love purely. Our wills have settled on the self like birds belimmed on branches, ready for the hunter.

John Wesley's accusations notwithstanding, Law never thought that the answer was to "try harder." *A Serious Call* is full of admonitions and exhortations, appeals to our intentions, but Law knew that insofar as our will inclines toward God with any integrity at all, something more has happened than us pulling our socks up. The ground of our willing has changed; it has a new source. The exposition of this change, which is a change in loving, is a principal focus of Law's later writings:

> All the Mysteries of Religion, and the Necessity of the whole
> Process of *Christ* in our Redemption . . . are all of them only
> for this one End; to help fallen Man to have a working Will
> towards that first Life, which he has lost. (*DK* 148)

The exhortations of *A Serious Call* have not lost their importance; rather, Law made them central to his teaching "of the whole Process of *Christ*." This "process of Christ" issues in the "new birth," that "regeneration" of humanity which is the recovery of wholeheartedness, the renewal of love: "Hell and Death, Curse and Misery, can never cease or be removed from the Creation till the *Will of the Creature is again* as it came from God and is only *a Spirit of Love* that willeth nothing but Goodness" (*SL* 363). "My will," "trying harder," cannot achieve this, not least because the will's being *mine* is the problem. My intentions are hopelessly egocentric. On the other hand, unless it is I that love, unless it is *my* loving, I disappear altogether and God's loses the beloved to whom he called in the twilight, "Adam, where are thou?" How can my willing be freed from me and remain mine?

Since Law shares the contemporary enthusiasm for Nature, he finds helpful analogies in plants. Plants grow in response to their environment. They turn toward the sun, take nutrients from the soil, absorb water, and through all this fulfill their "inclination" toward growth and growth into a particular kind of plant. As Law puts it, the plant is "a Growth from the Powers of the Sun, Stars, and Elements, upon the working Will in the Seed" (*DK* 165). We would call this process "organic," but Law, taking a cue from Boehme, calls it, rather boldly, "magical." Law's spokesman here, Theophilus, apologizes for any alarm or anxiety that the term may cause, though Law's critics probably were less "frighted" than convinced that he had lost his mind. A "magical" world, however, is Law's alternative to a "mechanical" one. "Magic" refers us not to conjuration or crones leaping around frog-filled cauldrons but rather to "the working power of the Will." It only implies "that the *Will*, whether in God, or the Creature, is the Ground and Seed of every Thing; is the generating working Power . . . and therefore Eternity and Time are magical; and Magic is, and must be, the Mother of all Things" (*DK* 149). Created beings are the fruit of God's intentions, down to the most exact and tiny detail, to the hairs on heads and the feathers on sparrows. Everything that exists is loved into being and sustained by love. "Magic," though, means still more than this. "The Will, whether in God, *or the Creature*, is the Ground and Seed of every Thing" (*DK* 165 [my emphasis]). Plants do not have wills as humans and angels do, but they unfold from within, as they assimilate their environment, giving and receiving. As Law frequently reminds his readers, this is what being "in Nature" and "according to Nature" is all about. Plants, then, are entirely different from boxes and cupboards. They, too, are willed, but the willing is "external" to the object: the "*Carpenter* cuts Timber into various Shapes and Forms, and then joins one Piece to another"; a plant, however, is "magical" because "it is a Birth...generated from the working Will in the...Seed" (*DK* 161).

Where does all this take us, and what has it got to do with Jesus? Plants grow according to the opportunities provided by their environment. In Law's terms, the "working will" or "desire" of the plant inclines toward its environment and so forms itself in collaboration with what Nature offers. Nothing, Law insists, once again trying to capture for Christianity this culturally charged idea, can be anything that Nature does not permit. The "working will" realizes the creature's capacities for growth; Nature provides the terms and the limits within which that growth can take place. The same is true of human beings, only here, heaven and earth are at stake. What is humanity's proper environment? According to what Nature should the wills of men and women work? Adam's loving inclined to himself and to a creaturely world that he might manage for himself. As we have seen, the will curves upon itself and, burdening Nature with its insatiable desire, turns creation into "this world." Consequently, all the will can do is work a life according to this mortal, transient world and thus do violence to the image of God, being self-contradicted. "A Will, given up to earthly Goods, is as Grass with *Nebuchadnezzar*, and has one Life with the Beasts of the Field" (*SP* 104). Humanity's true environment, of course, is the love of the Triune God. The giving and receiving of that life, that Divine company, is our proper dwelling. As Adam and Eve, though, we hide from this life, hide even as that "inspoken Word" stirs up our longing and even as the world disappoints us.

On the one hand, every creature, according to Law, possesses a "will," an inclining, through which it realizes its individual life; on the other hand, that "working will" operates in collaboration with a particular environment, by exploiting and responding to its surroundings. To flourish, the creature has to venture itself upon those surroundings.

> Wherever, and in whatever, the *working* Will chooseth to
> *dwell* and *delight*, that becomes the Soul's *Food*, its *Condi-
> tion*, its *Body*, its *Clothing*, and *Habitation*: For all these are
> the true and certain Effects and Powers of the working Will.
>
> (*SP* 104–5)

Thus, at all levels life involves something analogous to "trust,"
and Law makes the connection between this "willing" and
"faith."

> Faith … is that *Power by which a Man gives himself up to
> anything, seeks, wills, adheres to, and unites with it, so that
> his Life lives in it and belongs to it.* (DK 169–70)

The human tragedy, therefore, is one of exile. We are unable to
give ourselves up wholeheartedly, with complete trust, to the environment for which we were created. Our desire is hopelessly
divided and so, as our willing cannot work according to our true
environment, we do not live in accordance with it. Our making
was in the Son of God, who eternally offers himself to the Father, who, according to Law's analogy of the "three properties,"
is the Light that comes from the Father and eternally unites with
him through the Spirit. The sustaining environment, therefore, to
which we are called is the love that passes between the Father and
the Son and in which creation is offered, blessed, and received. We
return from the pinched constraints of "this world" as the Son's
love of the Father is raised in us by the Spirit. "And because ye are
sons, God hath sent forth the Spirit of his Son into your hearts,
crying, Abba, Father" (Gal. 4:6). Then, too, we reenter creation,
seeing it again through the shadows of its "frustration" and hearing its "groaning." We are free, and the nonhuman creation itself
is freed only as, through the Spirit, our willing is taken up into
the Son's. This is regeneration: we are born again into the love
that the Son offers the Father. We love in and through that love
with which the Son loves the Father, the love that is the Spirit.

The Son's will, therefore, incorporates our own, and because we are created in the eternal Son, the Son can fix our willing in his without our willing ceasing to be ours. My will — my love — is mine, never more so, since this is the environment for which I am created, yet my will is now more than mine, inspired, united, and borne up within a larger will. As Paul put it, "I live, yet not I, but Christ liveth in me" (Gal. 2:19). This is "truly only a Growth of Life, or magical Birth from the Powers of Father, Son, and Holy Ghost, upon the working Will in the Soul" (*DK* 162). What we need, then, is to come into this new beginning of love. But how?

Quenching Hell

The mythological narratives that Law has combined and retold, from "Eternal Nature" to the "inspoken Word," have their focus in a particular parcel of flesh and blood, living at a particular time and place: Jesus of Nazareth. Jesus, as we have noted before, is what they are about. The story of the fall tells of a beginning that is always present. This is who we are; our individual histories, our thoughts, words, feelings, and actions originate here, out of the will's preference of the self to God. What we need is a new start, a new origin, and one that does not recede in time but rather is always near, always beginning, always the source of life. God, though, in creating this world, this humanity out of Eternal Nature, pledged his faithfulness to our particular history, to the sorry way we have plodded through time and space. There is no going back, and if there is to be a way forward, it has to come from within this history, from one who is on the long march with us. A Savior who asked us, from the ease of an unfleshed heaven, to despair of history, to reject the flesh and leave behind the burdened world would not be faithful as God is faithful. What we need is a new Adam, and it is through this Pauline theme that William Law understands Jesus. He summarizes it all in *An Appeal to All That Doubt*:

> Here God, the second person in the Holy Trinity, took
> human nature upon him, became a suffering, dying man,
> that there might be found a man, whose sufferings, blood
> and death had power to extinguish the wrath and hell that
> sin had brought forth, and to be a fountain of the first
> heavenly life to the whole race of mankind.[18]

We are likely to read the description "a suffering, dying man" as
referring to the crucifixion. Law, however, is very clear that this
phrase characterizes the whole of Jesus' life. Many theologians,
as well as many preachers, tend to privilege either Christmas, the
feast of the incarnation, or Good Friday, the day of the cross. Law
warns against that. Among those that he has particularly in mind,
Jesus' teaching was elevated above his embarrassingly irrational
miracles; his moral example was treasured above the cross, while
the latter became a heroic death more worthy than an ascension
into heaven that was entirely "beyond reason."

> To ascribe our deliverance from sin, or the remission of our
> sins more to the life and actions, than to the death of Christ,
> or to his death more than to his resurrection and ascen-
> sion, is directly contrary to the plain letter and tenor of the
> scripture.[19]

The eternal Son takes human life, body and soul, and within that
entire human life, he works salvation. The whole life of Jesus,
therefore, is "for our salvation," not just the cross, and not just
the incarnation itself. The Sermon on the Mount, the precocious
child left in the temple, the calling of the disciples, the tiredness in
the boat, the party with publicans, the dead boy raised at Nain,
Gethsemane — it is all "for our salvation."

What is Jesus up to? If this whole life is a "work," what is
being done? The first thing that Law makes us see is "suffering."
As the new Adam, Jesus takes on the flesh of the old; he is bone
of our human bone, an Israelite within Israel within the Roman

Empire. He was not spared this difficult world. He "suffers" it. That means pain, of course, and what goes with our bodily life: hunger, weariness, the sore need for shelter and a kind welcome. More than that, though, Jesus suffers the world in that he struggles with it, he engages in a combat against sin and death: "every Kind of suffering and dying, that was a giving up, or departing from the Life of fallen Nature, was...necessary" (*SL* 449). The new Adam turns toward sorrow only because he must turn away from all the mortal securities that the world offers. He must have "nowhere to rest his head" except in the lap of God. Jesus brings "our fallen Nature...out of its *evil crooked* State" from within, through obedience to the Father, answering his call, rejecting violence, refusing possessiveness, forgiving enemies — through, in a word, the wholeheartedness of love. What has happened to the internal combat that Law describes so vividly, between preserving ourselves and communicating ourselves, between individuating and participating in multiple forms of life, between self-identity and the giving and receiving of community? This is the divided, contrary desire that issues in "whirling anguish," and it must be overcome in the new Adam if we are to find in him our restoration to peace. Jesus, then, receives himself from the Father, and as the image of God, he is able to participate in the world with the royal freedom of love: "As the Father hath loved me, so have I loved you" (John 15:9). Since he knows himself as entirely the gift of the Father, as living by the Spirit, the breath of the Father's mouth, he is so far free from himself as to be what the world needs, "The Son of Man [who] came not to be ministered unto, but to minister" (Mark 10:45).

That Law gives "suffering, dying" as his focal summary of Jesus' life should not surprise us. Christianity, he had told readers of *Christian Perfection*, "requireth a Renunciation of the World, and all worldly Tempers" (*CP* 36). Renunciation is the form of a Christian life. About this, Law never changed his mind. If it takes such renunciation to overcome the world, then, if Jesus is to free us, to whom the world clings intractable and deadly as ivy, Jesus' renunciation must be without reserve. He must be wholly one with us, "made like unto his brethren," so as in his own person to break the ties that bind us. He takes our place wholeheartedly and yet has no place in the world that we have made our home. Consequently, he is homeless, the violent world squeezing him out in suffering and dying: the crowds go home, friends disappear, disciples sleep, and he is crucified. As John's Gospel points out, as with the master, so with the disciple (John 13:16). Jesus forms us in himself, in the way freedom must go in the world, as "a Renunciation of the World, and all worldly Tempers." What goes by the name of "spirituality" today generally offers something more immediately cheerful. This just shows how needy we are for distraction from reality and how readily our culture provides it. On this side of glory, renunciation is uppermost. This is just honest; times of deep joy are rare. How could it be otherwise, trusting to a suffering, dying Savior, who welded together love of God and love of neighbor? We live on Holy Saturday, having just seen Easter on the tips of dawn's rose-red fingers. Nevertheless, all that being said, there is the other dimension, too, without which renunciation would just be a dry well and not, as it is, a means of receptivity, of "the quickening of a divine life." The suffering, dying Jesus also reveals God's glory. He is transfigured in unbearable light, triumphant over the mystery hidden from "the wise and prudent" but showed "unto babes" (Matt. 11:25). The Gospel stories exemplify the way of renunciation, but they also are the exegesis of divine love. As the new Adam, Jesus is the created face of God. The old Adam was meant to break out glories in Paradise; Jesus raises them here: sins are forgiven and the poor are blessed, there are healings, exorcisms, rejoicing mourners. The new environment, which is Jesus himself, begins to radiate and attract. A woman defies scorn to anoint Jesus' feet, a tax collector climbs a tree just to see him. Men and women are brought within the love of the Father and the Son, in the form that is God's embrace of our tragedy: the suffering servant who wages peace.

Still, Law knows that the cross does have a particular role as the fulfillment of Jesus' way of glory and renunciation. What goes on here, though, is beyond our imagination. Physical suffering is only the outward form of something much more sinister, a "descent into hell." This begins, Law tells us, in Gethsemane when "all the anguishing terrors of a lost soul began to open themselves in him."[20] In the wholeheartedness of his love for the Father, he experiences the horror of his absence, of the door shutting forever: "My God, my God, why hast thou forsaken me?" Jesus is "encompassed with that eternal death and sensibility of hell, which must have been the everlasting state of fallen man."[21] Among eighteenth-century Protestants, this interpretation of the cross was most familiar from the work of John Calvin. Calvin, though, argued that in this experience of hell, Jesus bore God's punishment for our sins. Jesus is punished in our place, as our substitute. Law wants to keep this profound insight into the inner meaning of the crucifixion but strongly rejects any explanation in terms of punishment. Punishment implies divine wrath, and divine wrath compromises divine love. Law will have nothing to do with teaching "an *infinite Resentment*, that could only be satisfied by an *infinite Atonement*" (*SL* 444). He must, therefore, substitute a different logic for that of punishment. He is not, however, altogether clear, relying rather on the emotional force of the "descent into hell" theme itself. To understand Law, we must first remember that it is only the body that holds Adam back from an immediate completion of the ruin, that hopeless "whirling anguish," into which his desire has brought him. If Jesus is "in all things" like us, save in the constancy of love, then he must be so to the very end that is ours, that has already fallen upon us. He must tread to its conclusion the way that we have made our own.

What, though, are the consequences of such community with us to the bitter end? Law hints at his answer when he tries to grapple with the traditional term *satisfaction*. Eusebius, the "very valuable and worthy Curate" in *The Spirit of Love*, pushes Theophilus over the familiar idea of Christ's death as making "satisfaction" for our sins. Law's response is to redefine "satisfaction" so as to remove any suggestion that Christ fulfills conditions for assuaging an angry God. He gives two interpretations. God's love is, first, insatiable love, unable to be satisfied until everything has been done to heal the beloved. This is "such a Love as could not be satisfied, till all that Glory and Happiness that was lost by the Death of Adam, was fully restored and regained again by the Death of Christ" (*SL* 436). Thus God is "satisfied." In terms of the tradition, this is a very cavalier response that ignores the way in which the concept of satisfaction has been used. It gives us a clue, though. Love, as Law has told us, is indefatigable in seeking to do good, to enter the presence of the beloved. The eternal Son goes to the furthest point of the "far country," brings even our rejection of God, our infinite loneliness, into the love between Father and Son. The utterly outside, to which masters in the parables cast foolish virgins and unworthy servants, "where there is wailing," is taken inside, where love restores in resurrection.

Eusebius does not entirely fall for satisfaction redefined in terms of the "Love...that wanted to have *full Satisfaction*." He protests, "But is there not some good Sense, in which Righteousness or Justice may be said to be *satisfied* by the Atonement and Sacrifice of Christ?" (*SL* 436). Theophilus's reply is equally wide of the tradition, but it gives us another clue. This time it is we who need satisfaction. We are, Law argues, deeply, wretchedly unsatisfied until that "Righteousness or Justice" that belongs to us is restored. When we recover goodness, our hearts will be satisfied. Law points us to the demands of our calling. We have betrayed it, and we do so again and again. Hell has no postal address; it is everywhere in the forsakenness that we have made for ourselves. It is the loss of those who miss themselves. What can quench this hell? Cynicism can harden us for a while; distraction generally does the job better still. Only faithfulness, though, can really quench hell, since unfaithfulness created it. Jesus hangs in despair; he hangs but still offers himself, still loves in this darkest of nights. So, when the centurion looks up and says, "Truly, this man was the Son of God," he says so much more than he knows. Humanity has returned to faithfulness. The new Adam has kept faith in the agony of the old. All those who are "in Christ" are incorporate with this faith.[22]

Jesus has reversed the way of Adam into the far country. Using a term from the second-century theologian Irenaeus, we say that Jesus "recapitulates," goes over the ground again. He lives the relationship of God and humanity but brings it to a better end. What remains to be asked in more detail, though, is how Law understands our participation in Christ's work. *How* do we come to share in Christ's benefits? Here we return to the "inspoken Word" or "seed of Christ." The particular way in which Law uses the idea should now be clearer. Although he generally treats the terms as if they were synonymous, "inspoken Word" and "seed of Christ" involve different metaphors that refer us to different aspects of God's grace as it is universally present within humanity.[23] "Inspoken Word" suggests that grace is a speaking, an interior voice. *The Spirit of Prayer* begins with one of Law's favorite metaphors: "The greatest Part of Mankind...may be said to be asleep." The "inspoken Word" is the voice that wakes up the sleeper, and because it is the inspoken word of Christ, it speaks in response to Moses and the prophets, and, finally and fully, in response to Jesus. The metaphor of the "seed of Christ," on the other hand, suggests a capacity. Our vocation is to be formed in Christ, therefore within the bond of love between the Father and the Son. This vocation, however, is not alien to us: it is an abiding gift within our being, we are made for this, it is within us as a capacity for this destiny. This destiny is not automatic or inevitable, and when we bring the metaphor "inspoken Word" alongside that of "seed," we remember that this capacity is a gift that we might not have received: it is within us, it makes us who we are, and yet it is not "of us" but rather is like a voice breaking in upon sleep. Our being is a gift further graced, "grace upon grace" (John 1:16).

The metaphor of the "seed" shapes Law's answer to the question "How do we benefit from Jesus' life, death, and resurrection?" For St. Paul, as for Law, Adam is the ancestor from whom we all descend. Paul, though, from whom the theme of the "old" and the "new" Adam derives, also speaks of Adam as a "sphere" or "context" to which we belong and from which we derive our fate: "As in Adam all die, even so in Christ shall all be made alive" (1 Cor. 15:22). Law adopts this and interprets it through his main apologetic concept, "Nature." No challenge seemed more sinister to Law than a theology that opposed "Nature" to "revelation" and "reasoning according to Nature" to "mysteries" and "dogmas." The Deists took this to generally unpopular extremes, but, as we have seen before, they did so riding on a widely shared cultural enthusiasm for investigation into Nature and for the intellectual clarity, order, and simplicity that such science brought.

> O unprofuse magnificence divine!
> O wisdom truly perfect! thus to call
> From a few causes such a scheme of things.[24]

At a time of such cultural confidence, the contrast between orderly Nature, whose laws were becoming matters of agreement and demonstration, and truths of revelation — mysterious, hard to articulate, and the cause of so much acrimony among Christians — was seductive. Law recognized, though, that even the beginnings of an opposition here threatened Christian faith with fragmentation and a reductive conformity to "natural reason." Is there a "religion of Nature"? Yes, answers Law, but it is Christianity with its mystery that passes understanding. Law seeks to show then that through the "seed of Christ," God operates as he always does: "according to Nature." But then, there is more in Nature than is dreamt of in a Deist's philosophy.

In order for a creature to grow, there must be a fit between the creature and its environment. Nothing can develop beyond what the environment makes possible; conversely, no environment can be formative unless the creature has a capacity to adapt to it, take what it needs, make its way within it. As fallen creatures, we are "in Adam" — that is, in an environment that holds out a range of possibilities for flourishing, none of which answer to our Divine vocation but all of which may attract our desire. Our wills, divided though they are, belong in this environment; they find satisfactions within it, exploit it and adapt to its terms. This environment poses grave limits; no "heavenly life," in Law's phrase, can prosper here. God, however, did not allow Adam and Eve to pass into this environment without fitting them, hiddenly, for a very different "Nature." He gave them the "seed," the capacity to be in Christ: "the *hidden Treasure* of every human Soul, . . . immured under Flesh and Blood . . . till it changes the Son of an earthly Adam into a Son of God" (*SL* 407). No seed, though, can grow without the proper environment. As the new Adam, Jesus creates that environment in our history, which is where we need it. More exactly, he *is* that environment. The plant turns toward the light, and our hearts turn toward the light of Christ as it shone in Israel and shines in the Scriptures and in the church, which is his body. Inward and outward, universal seed and historical incarnate Christ, are brought together in an analogy that holds throughout creation:

> Inwardly Man has a *Seed* of the Divine Life given into the Birth of his Soul. . . . Outwardly he has *Jesus Christ*, who as a *Sun* of Righteousness, is always casting forth his enlivening Beams on this *inward Seed*, to kindle and call it forth to the Birth, doing that to this Seed of Heaven in Man, which the

Sun in the Firmament is always doing to the vegetable Seeds in the Earth. (*SP* 32)

In this way, we "come to ourselves," and our "working wills" are united with the Son's eternal will of love for the Father.

As we have seen, "faith," according to Law, is "that *Power by which a Man gives himself up to anything, seeks, wills, adheres to, and unites with it, so that his Life lives in it and belongs to it*" (*DK* 169–70). Christian faith, therefore, is giving of oneself to be "in Christ." Such giving, though, would not be possible unless God had made us capable of thriving within his Triune life. In assuming humanity, in bearing our suffering, reworking the way of the old Adam, and in his resurrection, the Son has made himself the environment in which his own seed, our fittedness for him, may flourish. Law can insist, therefore, that Christ is "naturally" the "quickener" of life in us, our proper environment, and that God has done nothing except "in a *natural* Way, or according to the Nature of Things." Which, of course, Law adds, with a wink at his rogues' gallery, "must be *mysterious* to Man, because it is doing something *more* and *higher* than his Senses or Reason ever saw done" (*SL* 153 [my emphasis]). In the context of Law's culture, the conclusion is delightfully paradoxical: outside Christianity "man can have no Religion that is *sufficiently natural*; that is to say, no Religion that is sufficient, or equal to the Wants of his Nature" (*SL* 153).

Law's practical treatises demand change with the goal of nothing less than "perfection." There is one Christianity, and perfection is its standard. "Men in *Cloisters* and religious retirements cannot add more, and . . . Christians in all states of the world must not be content with less" (*SL* 153). For this, Law was accused of legalism and of laying insupportable burdens on perfectly decent people. He had cast "a noxious and baleful shade o'er all the comforts of life."[25] What is at stake here, for William Law at least, is whether our lives, even in intention, match the meaning that we give to the word *God*. The serious content of the word concerns an intimately present, inexhaustible, and holy reality, One from whom we receive everything moment by moment and fits us to be "partakers of the Divine nature."[26] Our response, advocated, Law argues, from all too many pulpits, is that we do our best. In truth, that is fated to amount to little: attend church as dutiful, worshipful English men and women and leave God to do the dramatic stuff when we die. In short, our response is not serious. Despite the rigors of the demand for perfection, though, in his practical treaties Law finds ways to maintain that demand while appealing to a gradual process sustained by the mercy of God. Reading Jacob Boehme inspired Law to a rich account of that process as the universal work of Divine love. Yet, the urgency does not slacken:

> There is no Peace, nor ever can be for the Soul of Man but in the Purity and Perfection of its first created Nature; nor can it have its Purity and Perfection in any other Way than in and by the *Spirit of Love*.[27]

The love of God is voracious and will not share sovereignty: "The Spirit of Love is not in you...till you live *freely, willingly, and universally* according to it."[28] Law anticipates the obvious objection that this is simply impossible, and he rejects it as firmly as he did in *Christian Perfection*:

> Nothing impure or imperfect in its Will and Working, can have any Union with God. Nor are you to think that these Words, the *Purity* and *Perfection* of God, are too high to be used on this Occasion...whatever [is] not thus, is at *Enmity* with God, and cannot have any Union of Life and Happiness with him, and in him. (*SL* 365)

Dr. Trapp attacked Law as being dangerously unrealistic, for promoting practices that hardened the dissolute against religion and discouraged the amiably devout. Law flips this accusation back on the accuser. The "world-renouncing" advocate of perfection rejects the compromises of Trapp's "good enough" Christianity because it takes seriously neither the world nor God's faithfulness. Eternal love does not wait for our arrival at death's door; it penetrates a creation that was, from the beginning in "Eternal Nature," made as its medium. The text on the title page of *A Serious Call* echoes to the end of Law's career: "Behold, I come quickly, and my reward is with me" (Rev. 22:12). The demand and promise of "perfection" must be the horizon within which we live because we have, in Christ, been taken up into perfect love. The Triune love of God is the environment that reconciles creation and perfects it.

The subtitle to *The Spirit of Prayer* is *The Soul Rising Out of the Vanity of Time, into the Riches of Eternity.* Christians live, Law tells us, in two worlds: we are "in Adam," under the conditions of the fall, and we are "in Christ," having been brought within the sphere of heaven. The "heavenly world" was always hidden within us but irrecoverable until Christ awakened our desire and formed us to his influence. The two "worlds," two spiritual ecosystems, cannot flourish together; one of them must diminish.

> All the Religion of fallen Man, all the Methods of our Redemption, have only this *one End*, to take from us that *strange* and *earthly* Life we have gotten by the Fall, and to kindle again the life of God and Heaven in our Souls.
>
> (*SP* 99)

In Christ, we are dying to the hopeless "vanity of time" as the heavenly world rises within us. Living in unbroken and wholehearted love of the Father, Christ established new conditions under which human life might flourish into its original calling. God promised his faithfulness to men and women, and so this new creation is made within time and in flesh and blood. Shaping, forming, influencing, giving and receiving, this new environment, as any "system of Nature," forces out that which cannot survive within it. The living connectivity of this environment, the energy of all its mediations of growth and change, the power that unites its diversity, is the Holy Spirit, incorporating us into Christ and, therefore, into the reciprocal flows of the Divine love.

> The Spirit of Prayer, is a *pressing forth* of the Soul out of this earthly Life; it is a stretching with all its Desire after the Life of God; it is a leaving, as far as it can, all its *own Spirit*, to receive a Spirit from above, to be one Life, one Love, one Spirit with Christ in God. (*SP* 104)

The media of this life, the means through which we thrive into God, are Scripture, the church, sacraments, prayer, deeds of love, teaching, and also the writings of such as Jacob Boehme and the counsel of Law's spokesman, Theophilus.

Toward the end of *The Spirit of Love*, Law takes up the question of our part in formation. How is this plant to lean toward to the sun? How may we turn to Christ so as to be as immediately in his presence, within his blessed influence, as were the "Publicans, Sinners, and Heathens" who seek him out in the Gospel stories (*SL* 487)? Straightaway, in the person of Theophilus, Law throws what might be called a devotional curveball. He tells Theogones that there is absolutely nothing to be gained from "Rules, Methods, and Contrivances" (*SL* 487). *A Serious Call*, though, is full of such methodical suggestions and promises great things from simply bringing even a single behavior under the discipline of a rule. Is Law now waving good-bye to all that discipline of spiritual militancy? At other points in the dialogues, his fall guy, Academicus, receives a mugging in love for trying to read himself to heaven. Now, though, Law's renunciation of helps and aids is much more sweeping. There is no help in them; indeed, "there is no Help but from a *total Despair*" of all such help (*SL* 490). Is Law including the church, one wonders, the preaching, the sacraments, prayers and worship, the very book that his readers have in their hands? His next move seems, if anything, still less comforting: we are solely to give ourselves up to the virtues of *"Patience, Meekness, Humility* and *Resignation to God."* If it all comes down to this, is not John Wesley vindicated at the last? What am I to do to claw my way through the crowd to Jesus, to get his attention? I am to be good. I am to try harder at those virtues, the very ones that, like Tantalus's grapes, recede from me every time I reach out for them? This is impossible, and Law knows it: "Consider only this, that to be *angry* at our own Anger, to be *ashamed* of our own Pride, and *strongly* resolve not to be *weak*, is the Upshot of all *human Endeavours;* and yet all this is rather the Life, than the Death of Self" (*SL* 490).

I am, of course, barking up the wrong tree, and the final pages of *The Spirit of Love* are as rich a response to Wesley as Law had given since May 14, 1738, when the methodical preacher's complaining letter arrived on the doorstep. The consideration that sets us off in another direction is that Law is not interested in *our* "Patience, Meekness, Humility, and Resignation to God." These qualities turn out not to be a cluster of higher virtues, at least not primarily. "Patience, Meekness, Humility, and Resignation to God" is a name. Even more than a description, it is a name for Jesus. By telling us to turn toward "Patience, Meekness, Humility, and Resignation to God," Law refers us "directly" to the "true Lamb of God." "For if I ask you, what the Lamb of God is, and means, must you not tell me ... the *Perfection* of Patience, Meekness, Humility, and Resignation to God?" (*SL* 488). These "virtues" are the form of Christ, or, rather, since his life defines these virtues, he shapes them to his own form. They are the glory in which Divine love appears — in Blake's words, the "human form divine."[29] If we desire the One set before us in the Gospels, we desire "Patience, Meekness, Humility, and Resignation to God" made perfect.

Law has already told us that "faith" and "desire" name the same reality from different angles. Faith is that trust in which we give ourselves over to that which we desire. To turn to these four excellencies, therefore, is not to take them to ourselves and try to achieve them; rather, we are to give ourselves over to them, and we can only do that because they name a person, a "working will," who draws, adapts, fits, and shapes us to them. In us, Christ works his form, a particular expression of his "nature."

> While you shut up yourself in Patience, Meekness, Humility, and Resignation to God, you are in the very Arms of Christ, your whole Heart is his Dwelling-Place, and He lives and works in you, as certainly as he lived in, and governed that Body and Soul, which he took from the Virgin *Mary.*
>
> (*SL* 488)

Christ has brought us within the operations of the Trinity: "You look for all your Salvation through the *Father*, working Life in your Soul by his *own Word*, and *Spirit*, which dwell in Him, and are one Life, both in Him and you" (*SL* 493). If this is the case, how could we put stock in devices and disciplines of our own devising? Or even of prayers, preaching, the fellowship of Christians, insofar as we imagine that they might of themselves usher us into a grace that Christ has already brought us? What we must do is trust, "sink down" into Christ.

Another problem crops up at this point. Theophilus himself provokes it. He urges Theogones with respect to trusting solely in the Lamb of God, forming us in his image:

> Stand, therefore, steadfastly...let nothing else enter into your Mind, have no other Contrivance, but everywhere, and in every Thing, to nourish and keep up *this State* of Heart.
>
> (*SL* 491)

Exhortations to "keep up" a "State of Heart" are risky. If we cannot advance ourselves through laboriously cultivating our own virtues, perhaps we can at least have the proper "feelings." I was prayed for by two well-meaning gentlemen who punctuated their petitions by asking me what I was feeling. Allow yourself to feel, they insisted. What is God doing in you — open yourself — how are you feeling? I found it difficult to feel on command. I was torn, though, between a reluctance to disappoint them — or, for that matter, have them think that I was beyond reviving, a one-man "burnt over" region — and a nervousness about lying in the house of God. I settled for owning to a warm glow, justified, in a pinch, by my having my back to a spotlight. Law warned against this elevation of the heartfelt. What are we risking by asking folk "*when*, and *where* they *felt* their Sins were forgiven them? When and where they *felt* Christ to take an entire Possession of them?"[30] We are, Law argues,

> hastening, and stirring up People to seek for Self-Justification, and compelling them to *think highly*, and affirm *rashly* of themselves. . . . Is not this making Faith in *one's self*, as good, as necessary, and as beneficial to us, as Faith in *Christ*?[31]

Not that this makes strong feeling something to be avoided or mocked. There is no greater virtue in coolness or a stiff upper lip. The Holy Spirit may well give us "particular *Impressions*, strong *Influences*, delightful *Sensations*, or heavenly *Foretastes* in the inward Man." We are to be grateful and see them for what they are: encouragements and incitements, "as *beneficial*, and *useful* to us in our spiritual Life, as other Blessings of God, such as Prosperity, Health, happy Complexion, and the like."[32] Advice to keep up this "State of Heart" is, then, troubling counsel, and Theogones challenges it.

> Permit me to mention a Fear that rises up in me. Suppose I should find myself so overcome with my own Darkness and selfish Tempers, as not to be able to *sink* from them into a Sensibility of this meek, humble, patient, full Resignation to God, what must I then do, or how shall I have the Benefit of what you have taught me? (*SL* 491)

Theophilus, however, is far from measuring faith by intensities of feeling or, for that matter, from measuring faith at all. Faith, he says, shows itself most clearly for what it is when our minds are in turmoil, or when we are swept with decidedly unholy feelings, or when we are just dull. You may "*stand turned*" to patience, humility, and resignation without feeling patient, humble, or resigned, indeed, with "no comfortable *Sensibility*" of doing any such thing. Faith is the yoke of Jesus, who says, "Come unto me, all ye that labor and are heavy laden, and I will refresh you" (Matt. 11:28). Here, we can see the use of means again: saying the Lord's Prayer, reading a psalm, complaining to God, lighting a candle, a whispered plea, asking for intercession, sitting outside a church. Once, I was so wretched that all I could do was half-heartedly make a cross on my forehead before I went to sleep. These things are not much, but they may be all that we can do, and, for Jesus, they are enough.

> Every sincere Wish and Desire, every inward Inclination of your Heart, that presses after these Virtues . . . is an *immediate direct* Application to Christ, is *worshipping* and *falling down* before him, is *giving up* yourself unto him, and the very *Perfection* of Faith in him. (*SL* 488)

He needs very little room in which to work.

Where have we gotten to? Law has been putting matters in the right order. He has sketched the "economy" of our lives as he has expounded the larger economy of creation, fall, and redemption. We begin with Christ, whose attraction stirs our love, the love that is his own stirring within us. We trust this life that radiates toward us; perhaps we do not trust very much, just a peep out from the self's snail shell, just the length of a mustard seed. It is enough, though, and the formation begins, and Christ will not stop his working until we have become his commentary on "Patience, Meekness, Humility, and Resignation to God." What about those rules, disciplines, times and places, and methods?

These, too, may now find their proper place in the economy of grace. Law's argument has taken rules and methods, all the good practices of *A Serious Call*, out of our hands and given them to Christ. They are good things, and not a few — the sacraments, the Scriptures, the fellowship of the body of Christ — are both commanded and commended to us by God. God, though, is free in his use of these. We do not know which words will start someone into life, which community will prove a fit environment for a surprising work of God, which actions will be fruitful. We pray and do and trust. And only sometimes, out of the corner of our eye, or when we look back from a way distant, may we glimpse, perhaps, the traces of his labor in us.

Something, though, something huge, is still missing. The form of Christ, Law tells us, and, therefore, the form of the Christian is "Patience, Meekness, Humility, and Resignation to God." Should it not be "love"? Perhaps, Law has all along, albeit unconsciously, been preaching up the self in disguise. Is not "Patience, Meekness, Humility, and Resignation to God" a recipe for the religious individual, content with inwardness, passive, a little melancholy, mostly disengaged, keeping a wary eye out for perturbing influences, steering clear of temptations, maintaining, as best she can, a fragile spiritual equilibrium? Not necessarily. Law's fourfold characterization repeats his summation of Jesus as the "suffering, dying" man, a description that points down the path that Jesus opens to us as the way to freedom. "Patience, Meekness, Humility, and Resignation to God" is not some individualistic spiritual cocoon but rather the face of the only freedom that matters. "My little children, let us not love in word, neither in tongue; but in deed and in truth" (1 John 3:18). Love can only be anything more than egocentric partiality, even when it is noble and apparently self-sacrificing, to the degree that we have made our exodus from the self.

> Look at every Vice, Pain, and Disorder in human Nature; it
> is in itself nothing else but the Spirit of the Creature turned

from the *Universality* of Love to some *self-seeking* or *own Will* in created Things. (*SL* 360)

The Lamb of God is what that departure from the self, the "own will," looks like, and those who worship him are those he has brought out with him, who have "washed their robes and made them white in the blood of the Lamb" (Rev. 7:14). This fourfold face of freedom is the liberated heart, the eye of the needle, the open space through which the love of God passes into the world. Our conflicted desire finds, at last, the room that it needs, which is nothing short of the eternal space of God, that *"unchangeable Will to all Goodness."* We were created for this, to will in and with the eternal will, to love in God's loving. God "can Will nothing in their Existence but that they should live and work and manifest that *same Spirit* of Love and Goodness which brought them into Being" (*SL* 360). Human energy, goodwill, practical intelligence, moral discipline cannot attain this. We cannot think or strive our way into this "Spirit of Love."

> The *Spirit of Love* is a Spirit of *Nature* and *Life;* and all the Operations of Nature and Life are according to the working Powers of Nature; and every Growth and Degree of Life can only arise in its *own* Time and Place from its *proper* Cause, and as the genuine Effect of it. (*SL* 380)

The Spirit of Love can come to us only as freedom, catching us up, blowing as it will, gathering our energies, our thoughts and actions, but not by our direction. They are ours, yet more than ours. "The Almighty brought forth all Nature for this only End, ... that Creatures ... might communicate the Spirit of Love and Goodness, give and receive mutual Delight and Joy to and from one another" (*SL* 365).

Prayer, as the desire in which we reach for God, like the plant seeks the sun, reaches its fullness when "it does not so much pray as live in God." Prayer is not constrained to times and places but rather is the stretching forth of "Resignation, to do and be, what and how his Beloved pleaseth" (*SP* 128). Once again, Law is trying to get matters in the right order, the proper economy. Love is free only through the foolishness of "Patience, Meekness, Humility, and Resignation to God." Godly action begins with what looks like a retreat from action. The freedom of charity, by which all is measured, lies in expecting nothing of ourselves but everything, even to the resurrection of the dead, from the God who is bringing us to life. So we must turn toward the world by turning away from it. But then, why should that be surprising? After all, Jesus, pinned immobile upon the cross, the epitome of pitiful inaction, is the fulcrum that turns everything around.

Everything, then, is to be expected from God, and Christ is the measure of our expectation. Looking to Jesus, crucified and risen, Christians find hope and learn for what to hope. In a particularly beautiful passage, Law urges,

> Ask what Christ is? He is the *universal Remedy* of all Evil broken forth in Nature and Creature.... He is the unwearied Compassion, the long-suffering Pity, the never-ceasing Mercifulness of God to every Want and Infirmity of human Nature. He is the Breathing forth of the Heart, Life, and Spirit of God, into all the dead Race of *Adam*. He is the Seeker, the Finder, the Restorer, of all that was lost and dead to the Life of God. He is the Love, that, from Cain to the End of Time, prays for all its Murderers; the Love that willingly suffers and dies among Thieves, that Thieves may have a Life with him in Paradise; the Love that visits Publicans, Harlots, and Sinners, that wants and seeks to forgive, where most is to be forgiven. (*SP* 108)

We have followed Law from the mystery of Eternal Nature, through fall, grace, creation, fall, and grace again, to the incarnate Word and to ourselves restored and set in the Way. What, though, is still to come? Most typically, Law expounds Christian hope in terms of the renewal of that perfection which we lost in Adam. This is too constrained a hope, though, to some extent, his excessive development of Adam's perfection forces him to it. Fortunately, Law's praise of Christ and of God's pursuit of his beloved creation intimates a fulfillment all the more glorious for the way taken, an eternal enjoyment of Divine love by a creation that bears testimony to the heights and depths of it. The praise of angels and humanity is in eternity a wonderment at the "Love that...wants and seeks to forgive, where most is to be forgiven." The Father has gathered up his cloak, said good-bye to ceremony, and scampered to hold the prodigal.

Who, though, will finally enjoy the feast of reconciliation? Law was no more interested in cheap hope than in cheap grace. He approaches the issue of universal salvation with some caution. There is a vital existential difference between hoping for the redemption of all, as a reflex of one's own knowledge of God's love, and indulging an expectation of it as a comfortable and reassuring "doctrinal" fact that eases the mind. This distinction, of course, has been with us all along: it is the difference between reliance on externals of reason or social practice and the inward operation of "a Life," a "working will." Any easygoing affirmation of "universalism" risks distracting us from reality, from the present struggle with evil, a struggle no less serious whatever hope we have. The bias of Law's thought on the matter, though, is plain enough. Law is furious over the notion that God from all eternity has decided that certain people will be damned. Those who hold this doctrine "so *blaspheme* God, as to make him from all Eternity *absolutely* to elect some to an *irresistible* Salvation, and absolutely to *reprobate* others to an unavoidable Damnation."[33] Surely this is merely the projection of human selfishness onto a holy God. More constructively, Law provided an alternative interpretation of the biblical language that supports the doctrine of predestination. He suggests that the stories of Cain and Abel, Jacob and Esau, Israel and Egypt, for instance, do not tell us about God's choice and rejection of specific people. These individual histories must be read *allegorically*. They concern God's rejection of humanity's self-destruction in sin and, correspondingly, his election of his own work, of the seed of Christ implanted in all:

> Here you have the whole *unalterable* Ground of Divine *Election* and *Reprobation;* it relates not to any particular Number of People or Division of Mankind, but solely to the two Natures that are, both of them, without Exception, in every Individual of Mankind. All that is earthly, serpentine, and devilish in every Man, is *reprobated* and *doomed* to Destruction; and the heavenly Seed of the new Birth in every Man, is *That* which is *chosen, ordained,* and *called* to eternal Life. (*SL* 463)

The stories of Isaac and Ishmael, David and Saul, point us to the contrary, embattled state of our lives. They also, though, provide a line of sight along which we may see the triumph of Christ, the chosen seed. However, lest we jump too readily for complacency, Law reminds us that, as to the biblical stories, "nothing is here to be understood personally, or according to the Flesh of these Persons on either Side" (*SL* 465). We are not, therefore, released from caution as to the fate of specific individuals.

In his final work, the *Address to the Clergy*, Law goes further by introducing a version of "purgatory." Divine love never abandons its purpose, though it never ceases to work as love either. Some, Law suggests, perhaps many, after death will continue to labor in self-destruction until, finally, God's love overcomes their pride and isolation:

> God's Providence, from the *Fall* to the *Restitution* of all Things, is doing the *same Thing*, as when he said to the dark Chaos of fallen Nature, "Let there be light"; He still says, and will continue saying the same Thing, till there is no Evil of Darkness left in all that is Nature and Creature.... And

if long and long *Ages* of fiery Pain, and tormenting Darkness, fall to the Share of many, or most of God's Apostate Creatures, they will last no longer, than till the great fire of God has melted *all Arrogance* into Humility, and all that is SELF has died in the long Agonies and Bloody Sweat of a lost God, which is that *all-saving* Cross of Christ, which will never give up its redeeming Power, till Sin and Sinners have no more a Name among the Creatures of God.[34]

Law extends the universality of God's salvation not only in "time," as he does here, but also with regard to "space." He takes up, that is, the issue of those outside any contact with the Christian church. He does not do this in any great detail, and his suggestion probably begs more questions than it answers. The proposal, though, however little he develops it, comes straight from his conviction that, despite Deist polemics, God does not arbitrarily choose one people and disregard all others. The "inspoken word," as we have seen, witnesses to and works toward Christ in all human beings. Christ within speaks, to be sure, in Moses and the prophets, but they are not his only prophets. From the "inspoken Word,"

> many eminent Spirits, Partakers of a Divine Life, have appeared in so many Parts of the heathen World; glorious Names, Sons of Wisdom, that shone, as Lights hung out by God, in the midst of idolatrous Darkness. These were the Apostles of a *Christ within.* (SP 33)

God has not left himself without witness. Nevertheless, even where Christ is not named, this witness is still a witness to Christ and not, as Deism had made it, to a God within the limits of common reason. How can this be? Law's hint is that, through a myriad of ways and witnesses, God awakens a desire that is nothing less than a desire for Jesus. Jesus, after all, is God enfleshed, and whosoever longs for a God like this loves Christ and will recognize him. In one description, Law blends together the figure of Jesus and the mystery of God, interpenetrating them, as one reveals the other:

> God is unwearied *Patience*, a *Meekness* that cannot be pro-
> voked; he is an ever-enduring *Mercifulness;* he is unmixed
> *Goodness*, impartial, universal *Love*....He is the *Good*
> from which nothing but Good cometh, and resisteth all Evil,
> *only* with Goodness. (*SP* 140)

Wherever human desire strains for this, there is the Spirit, groaning for Christ.

At the very end of his life, if we may accept Thomas Langcake's account, Law admitted that his hope had burst all bounds to include even the fallen angels.

> He said that not only the whole human race but even the
> fallen angels would all be delivered out of misery....He said
> that there would be *a chasm in creation*, without the angels
> being taken into happiness.[35]

We would completely misunderstand this universal hope if we did not see it as the completion of God's present way with us. Such a fulsome resurrection may be a completion beyond our imagining, but nonetheless, God does not wake to action only at the last, ours or creation's. The seed grows now, as our present lives turn toward the light, our hearts and minds take in Christ's nourishment, and our wills seek out all that he gives. Is it enough, though? Can the small beginnings that we know really issue in Law's vast hope? Rather, does not the world's woe, the persistence of war and violence, the evisceration of the earth's blessings, the wretchedness of grief, the ambiguities even of our best efforts, suggest that such hope is an illusion? To ask these questions, though, is to shift into the position that Law has taught us to recognize as the idle luxury of reason. Our only "evidence" is the desire that God has set going in us, the beauty that we have fallen for. To the anxious "Is it enough?" we have Jesus' reply:

> The kingdom of heaven is like to a grain of mustard seed, which a man took, and sowed in his field: Which indeed is the least of all seeds: but when it is grown, it is the greatest among herbs, and becometh a tree, so that the birds of the air come and lodge in the branches thereof. (Matt. 13:31–32)

In the end, Law's answer to the doubting, despairing, distracted, and evasive "old Adam" in each of us is not argument but rather the flames of love. So, in the end, Law compresses his teaching to seven words: "All Religion is the Spirit of Love" (*SP* 465).

Notes

Introduction

1. William Law, *A Serious Call to a Devout and Holy Life; The Spirit of Love*, ed. Paul G. Stanwood, with an introduction by Austin Warren and Paul G. Stanwood, and a preface by John Booty (New York: Paulist Press, 1978); Stephen Hobhouse, ed., *Selected Mystical Writings of William Law*, 2nd ed. (London: C. W. Daniel, 1940); A. Keith Walker, *William Law: His Life and Work* (London: SPCK, 1973).

1. "An Unhurried Life"

1. Gordon E. Rupp, *Religion in England, 1688–1792* (New York: Oxford University Press, 1986), 220.

2. Stephen Hobhouse identified this work as Law's initial introduction to Boehme ("Fides et Ratio: The Book Which Introduced Jacob Boehme to William Law," *Journal of Theological Studies* 37, no. 148 [October 1936]: 350–68).

3. Recalled from a conversation with Francis Okely, shortly before Law's death (Christopher Walton, *Notes and Materials for an Adequate Biography of the Celebrated Divine and Theosopher, William Law* [London: printed for private circulation, 1854], n. 426). The reference to Dr. Cheyne was noted by Law's friend the diarist John Byrom (Henri Talon, ed., *Selections from the Journals and Papers of John Byrom, Poet, Diarist, Shorthand Writer, 1691–1793* [London: Rockliff, 1950], 221).

4. Jacob Boehme, *The Way to Christ*, trans. Peter Erb, with an introduction by Peter Erb, and a preface by Winfried Zeller (New York: Paulist Press, 1978), 78.

5. Durand Hotham, *The Life of Jacob Behmen* (London: printed for H. Blunden, 1654), 5 (text is unpaginated).

6. William Law, *Some Animadversions upon Dr. Trapp's Late Reply, The Works of William Law*, vol. 6 (Eugene, OR: Wipf and Stock, repr., 2001), 108.

7. Arianism is an ancient heresy deriving from the teachings of Arius, a fourth-century presbyter in Alexandria, who argued that God the Father was alone eternal and that the Son was a creature, albeit the highest and most perfect creature, through whom God created the world. Arianism had a new lease on life in the eighteenth century, particularly as expounded by William Whiston, Newton's successor as Lucasian professor of mathematics at Cambridge, and by another Newtonian, Samuel Clarke, who had a considerable reputation both as a scientist and as a metaphysician. Clarke, in particular, argued that the classical doctrine of Christ as coequal with the Father was not supported by Scripture.

8. Cited in J. H. Overton, *William Law: Nonjuror and Mystic* (London: Longmans, Green, 1881), 181.

9. Law has, though, ancient precedent for the figure of Rusticus. Pope Gregory the Great (ca. 540–604), in his *Dialogues*, introduces Sanctulus, a holy but unlearned priest. Gregory notes, in words that Law might have used of Rusticus, "Compare, if you will, his learned ignorance with our own unlearned knowledge; his learning towers up while ours lies prone" (cited in Bernard McGinn, *The Growth of Mysticism: Gregory the Great through the Twelfth Century* [New York: Crossroad, 1999], 45).

10. John Wesley, *A Letter to the Reverend Mr. Law, Occasioned by Some of His Late Writings* (London, 1756), 19.

11. William Warburton was a pugnacious controversialist who eventually became bishop of Gloucester.

12. William Warburton, *The Divine Legation of Moses: In Nine Books* (4th ed.; 5 vols.; London: J. & P. Knapton, 1755), book I, part II, 322; book VI, 108–9.

13. William Law, *An Humble, Earnest, and Affectionate Address to the Clergy* (London: printed for M. Richardson, 1761), 65.

14. Ibid., 65–66.

15. Ibid., 70.

16. Richard Tighe, *A Short Account of the Life and Writings of the Late William Law, A.M.* (London: printed for the author, 1813), 12, 33.

2. All Law and No Gospel?

1. John Wesley, *The Works of John Wesley*, vol. 18, *Journals and Diaries I (1735–38)*, ed. W. Reginald Ward and Richard P. Heitzenrater (Nashville: Abingdon, 1988), 140, 325.

2. J. H. Overton, *William Law: Nonjuror and Mystic* (London: Longmans, Green, 1881), 83.

3. Ibid., 87–88.

4. *A Letter to Mr. Law: Occasion'd by Reading His Treatise on Christian Perfection; with a Copy of Verses, Address'd to the Same Author. By a Lover of Mankind* (London: printed for W. Hinchliffe, 1728), 22.

5. J. H. Overton, *William Law: Nonjuror and Mystic* (1881; repr., New York: Kessinger, 2003), 117.

6. Ibid.

7. Alister McGrath, *Iustitia Dei: A History of the Christian Doctrine of Justification*, 2nd ed. (Cambridge: Cambridge University Press, 1998), 188–226, 292–308.

8. Overton, *William Law*, 81.

9. Ibid., 85–86.

10. Here, "wants" in the sense of "lacks" or "needs."

11. "Flavia" is another use of Roman imperial rule as a symbol for worldliness. The Flavian family produced Vespasian, Titus, and Domitian, the last of this trio notable for his persecution of Christianity.

12. "Calidus" means "hot" — as we might say, "hot on every opportunity for profit."

13. Joseph Trapp, *The Nature, Folly, Sin, and Danger of Being Righteous Overmuch: The Substance of Four Discourses*, 4th ed. (London, 1739), 19.

14. *A Letter to Mr. Law*, 22.

15. Richard Tighe, *A Short Account of the Life and Writings of the Late William Law, A.M.* (London: printed for the author, 1813), 31. Tighe's book is rather slight, but he did have the benefit of speaking to some at King's Cliffe who remembered Law, though they must have been quite advanced in years at the time of those conversations or very young when Law was alive.

3. Devout and Holy ... and Reasonable?

1. Joseph Trapp, *The Nature, Folly, Sin, and Danger of Being Righteous Overmuch: The Substance of Four Discourses*, 4th ed. (London, 1739), 21.

2. Along with, and closely related to, "Nature," as we will see in chapter 7 especially.

3. Thomas Sprat, *The History of the Royal Society of London for the Improving of Natural Knowledge* (London: printed by T. R. for J. Martyn and J. Allestry, 1667), 3.

4. Abraham Cowley, "To the Royal Society," lines 116–19, 136–45.

5. James Thomson, "To the Memory of Sir Isaac Newton," lines 76–90.

6. Alexander Pope, "Epitaph Intended for Sir Isaac Newton in Westminster-Abbey."

7. William Law, *The Case of Reason; or, Natural Religion, Fairly and Fully Stated* (London: W. Innys, 1731), 132.

8. Abraham Cowley, "Reason: The Use of It in Divine Matters," lines 27–28, 31–32, 41.

9. Matthew Tindal, *Christianity as Old as the Creation; or, the Gospel a Republication of the Religion of Nature*, vol. 1 (London, 1730), 11. Tindal did complete the second volume of this work, leaving the manuscript in the hands of Edmund Gibson, bishop of London. Gibson, however, burned the work in order to protect Tindal's posthumous reputation.

10. Ibid., 30.

11. Law, *The Case of Reason*, 62.

12. Ibid.

13. Tindal, *Christianity as Old as the Creation*, 24.

14. Ibid., 63.

15. John Toland, *Christianity Not Mysterious; or, A Treatise Shewing That There Is Nothing in the Gospel Contrary to Reason, nor above It: and That No Christian Doctrine Can Be Properly Call'd a Mystery* (London, 1696).

16. Tindal, *Christianity as Old as the Creation*, 199.

17. Ibid., 12.

4. A Devout and Holy Day

1. Lewis Bayly, *The Practice of Pietie, Directing a Christian How to Walk That He May Please God* (Edinburgh: printed by Robert Young and Evan Tyler, 1642), 183–89, 192–94, 197–259.

2. Henry Bull, *Christian Praiers and Holie Meditations: As Wel for Priuate as Publique Exercise; Gathered Out of the Most Godly Learned of Our Time* (London: printed by R. Robinson for S. Waterson and N. Ling, 1596), 158–60, 163–64, 212–67.

3. I have remembered the phrase "ambulance work on words" from one of my first theology lectures, some thirty years ago, given by the late Sidney Hall Evans, then dean of King's College, London.

4. Far more, of course, have discovered him as a marvelously hateable villain in numerous radio, film, and television versions.

5. Charles Dickens, *David Copperfield* (London: Folio Society, 1984), 671.

6. John Locke, *Some Thoughts Concerning Education* (London: A & J Churchill, 1693), 6.

5. A Serious Call to the Gospel?

1. Dietrich Bonhoeffer, *The Cost of Discipleship* (New York: Touchstone, 1995), 43–44.

2. J. H. Overton, *William Law: Nonjuror and Mystic* (London: Longmans, Green, 1881); repr., New York: Kessinger, 2003), 81.

3. William Law, *Of Justification by Faith and Works: A Dialogue between a Methodist and a Churchman* (London: printed for J. Richardson), 2. Cf. James 2:17.

4. Ibid., 3.

6. The Great and Mysterious Story

1. Jacob Boehme, *Aurora, That Is, the Day-Spring; or, Dawning of the Day in the Orient or Morning-Rednesse in the Rising of the Sun* (London: printed by John Streater for Giles Calvert, 1656), 427.

2. Jacob Boehme, *On the Election of Grace and Theosophic Questions* (Whitefish, MT: Kessinger, 2007), 10.

3. J. H. Overton, *William Law: Nonjuror and Mystic* (London: Longmans, Green, 1881); repr., New York: Kessinger, 2003), 420.

4. "There is no one definition of myth, no Platonic form of a myth against which all actual instances can be measured. Myths... differ enormously in their morphology and their social function" (G. S. Kirk, *Myth: Its Meaning and Function in Ancient and Other Cultures* [Berkeley: University of California Press, 1970], 126).

5. For one such history, see Maurice Wiles, "Myth in Theology," in *The Myth of God Incarnate*, ed. John Hick (London: SCM Press, 1977), 148–66. As distinct from "mythology," "mythical," and "mythological," the word *myth* was established in English usage only during the mid-nineteenth century, largely as a result of the debates over

David Friedrich Strauss's book *The Life of Jesus Critically Examined*, translated by George Eliot (1846). See Wiles, "Myth in Theology," 149.

6. John Creed, "Uses of Classical Mythology," in *The Theory of Myth: Six Studies*, ed. Adrian Cunningham (London: Sheed & Ward, 1973), 19 (my emphasis).

7. Margaret Dalziel, *Myth and the Modern Imagination* (Dunedin, NZ: University of Otago Press, 1967), 28.

8. John Milton, *Paradise Lost*, book 4, lines 495–97.

9. For one analysis of the cognitive functions of myth, see Ian Barbour, *Myths, Models and Paradigms: The Nature of Scientific and Religious Language* (London: SCM Press, 1974), chapter 2; and for a recent discussion of the importance of myth for theology and preaching, see Paul Avis, *God and the Creative Imagination: Metaphor, Symbol, and Myth in Religion and Theology* (New York: Routledge, 1999), chapter 11.

10. C. S. Lewis, *An Experiment in Criticism* (Cambridge: Cambridge University Press, 1992), 42–44.

11. K. K. Ruthven, *Myth* (London: Methuen, 1976), 71. In popular culture, the nameless monster in Mary Shelley's novel has so overshadowed the details of her story that he has assumed the surname of his fictional creator, Victor Frankenstein.

12. Thomas Hobbes, *Leviathan* (London: Penguin Books, 1968), 109–10.

13. Cited in Ruthven, *Myth*, 48.

7. The Father's House

1. For Law's use of the parable, see *SP* 46; *DK* 95, 111.

2. John Wesley, *A Letter to the Reverend Mr. Law, Occasioned by Some of His Late Writings* (London, 1756), 39.

3. This certainly is the principal teaching. In *An Appeal to All That Doubt*, however, Law conflates "Eternal Nature" with the kingdom of heaven — that is, the realm of the original angelic creation. The later writings make clear the important distinction.

4. William Law, *An Appeal to All That Doubt or Disbelieve the Truths of the Gospel, The Works of William Law*, vol. 6 (Eugene, OR: Wipf and Stock, repr., 2001), 125. William Law, *Some Animadversions upon Dr. Trapp's Late Reply, The Works of William Law*, vol. 6 (Eugene, OR: Wipf and Stock, repr., 2001).

5. Christopher Walton, *Notes and Materials for an Adequate Biography of the Celebrated Divine and Theosopher, William Law* (London: printed for private circulation, 1854), 409n.

6. John Freke, *A Treatise on the Nature and Property of Fire. In Three Essays: I. Shewing the Cause of Vitality, and Muscular Motion; with Many Other Phaenomena; II. On Electricity; III. Shewing the Mechanical Cause of Magnetism; and Why the Compass Varies in the Manner It Does* (London: printed for W. Innys and J. Richardson, 1752), 2, 7, 37.

7. Ibid., 19–24; John Freke, *An Essay to Shew the Cause of Electricity, and Why Some Things Are Non-Electricable; in a Letter to Mr. William Watson, F.R.S.*, 2nd ed., with an appendix (London: printed for W. Innys, 1746), 4–6.

8. Freke, *The Nature and Property of Fire*, 32–34.

9. This became a significant concern in late twentieth-century theology. For two now classic statements, see Karl Rahner, *The Trinity* (London: Burns & Oates, 1970); Jürgen Moltmann, *The Trinity and the Kingdom of God: The Doctrine of God* (London: SCM Press, 1981).

10. John Tillotson, *A Seasonable Vindication of the Blessed Trinity, Being an Answer to This Question: Why Do You Believe the Doctrine of the Trinity?* (London: printed for B. Aylmer, 1697), 11.

11. John Tillotson, *A Sermon on Concerning the Unity of the Divine Nature and the Blessed Trinity* (London: printed for B. Aylmer and W. Rogers, 1693), 51–56.

12. James Foster, *The Usefulness, Truth, and Excellency of the Christian Revelation Defended against the Objections Contain'd in a Late Book, Intitled, Christianity as Old as the Creation, &c.* (London: printed for J. Noon, 1734).

13. Law, *An Appeal to All That Doubt*, 125.

14. Ibid., 107.

15. Edwin A. Burtt, *The Metaphysical Foundations of Modern Science*, rev. ed. (Garden City, NY: Doubleday, 1952), 173.

16. For more examples, see Richard S. Westfall, *The Construction of Modern Science: Mechanisms and Mechanics* (Cambridge: Cambridge University Press, 1977), chapters 2, 6; Carolyn Merchant, *The Death of Nature: Women, Ecology, and the Scientific Revolution* (San Francisco: Harper & Row, 1980), 164–235.

17. Merchant, *The Death of Nature*, 216–27.

18. Robert Boyle, *A Free Enquiry into the Vulgarly Received Notion of Nature*, ed. Edward B. Davis and Michael Hunter, Cambridge Texts in the History of Philosophy (Cambridge: Cambridge University Press, 1996), 40.

19. Cited in Burtt, *The Metaphysical Foundations of Modern Science*, 186, 196.

20. Boyle, *Free Enquiry*, 12–13.

21. Arnold O. Benz, "Culture in a New Scientific Worldview," *Journal of Interdisciplinary Studies* 17, no. 1/2 (2005): 124. See also Steven Best and Douglas Kellner, *The Postmodern Turn* (New York: Guildford Press, 1999), 203–7.

22. Merchant, *The Death of Nature*, 275. Newton himself, though, continued to acknowledge the limits of mechanistic philosophy and, therefore, of the explanatory adequacy of his own theories (see Merchant, *The Death of Nature*, 283–87).

23. Alexander Pope, "Essay on Man," epistle I, lines 289–94, in Alexander Pope, *Poetical Works*, ed. Herbert Davis, Oxford Standard Authors (Oxford: Oxford University Press, 1978), 249.

24. Boyle, *Free Enquiry*, 12.

25. If anything, the Greek favors Law's own doctrine of "from Eternal Nature," as in the Jerusalem Bible translation: "It is by faith that we understand that the ages were created by a word from God, so that from the invisible the visible world came to be."

26. Merchant, *The Death of Nature*, 276.

27. Greg Bear, *Blood Music* (London: Gollancz, 1985), 262.

28. Ibid., 238–39.

8. The Way into the Far Country

1. Commentators are rather at sea as regards the glass. Where the detail is not just ignored, various proposals as to its meaning and origin are made, but none holds a consensus.

2. Jacob Boehme, *Mysterium Magnum*, 1:93.

3. For instance, Isaiah 14:12; Revelation 12:7.

4. William Law, *An Appeal to All That Doubt or Disbelieve the Truths of the Gospel*, *The Works of William Law*, vol. 6 (Eugene, OR: Wipf and Stock, repr., 2001), 128.

5. Samuel Taylor Coleridge, *Lectures, 1808–1819, on Literature*, ed. R. A. Foakes, The Collected Works of Samuel Taylor Coleridge 5 (Princeton, NJ: Princeton University Press, 1987), 2:315.

6. Law, *An Appeal to All That Doubt*, 69.

7. Ibid. (my emphasis).

8. William Law, *The Grounds and Reasons of Christian Regeneration, or the New Birth; Offer'd to the Consideration of Christians and Deists* (London: printed for W. Innys and R. Manby, 1739), 5.

9. Law, *Christian Regeneration*, 4 (my emphasis).

10. Law, *An Appeal to All That Doubt*, 69.

11. Ibid.

12. Fenelon, cited in Henri de Lubac, *The Mystery of the Supernatural*, trans. Rosemary Sheed (New York: Crossroad, 1998), 78.

13. Cajetan, cited in ibid., 29.

9. The Return of the Prodigal

1. William Law, *The Grounds and Reasons of Christian Regeneration, or the New Birth; Offer'd to the Consideration of Christians and Deists* (London: printed for W. Innys and R. Manby, 1739), 4.

2. Law, *Christian Regeneration*, 4–5.

3. St. John of the Cross, *The Living Flame of Love* 3.22.

4. Among earlier works, see Augustine's *City of God*. Although he does not mention either Law or Mandeville, the following discussion is indebted to John Milbank's persuasive argument in *Theology and Social Theory: Beyond Secular Reason*, 2nd ed. (Oxford: Blackwell, 2006).

5. Thomas Hobbes, *Leviathan* (London: Penguin Books, 1968), 186.

6. Ibid., 185.

7. Bernard Mandeville, *The Fable of the Bees or Private Vices, Public Benefits* (London: printed for J. Roberts, 1714), 28, 32.

8. Ibid., 160.

9. Ibid., 34.

10. William Law, *Remarks upon a Late Book, Entitled, "The Fable of the Bees," &c.*, in *The Works of the Reverend William Law, M.A.* (1892–1893; repr., Eugene, OR: Wipf & Stock, 2001), 2:6.

11. Mandeville, *The Fable of the Bees*, 22.

12. Law, *Remarks upon a Late Book*, 8.

13. William Law, *An Humble, Earnest, and Affectionate Address to the Clergy* (London: printed for M. Richardson, 1761), 7.

14. Catherine of Sienna, *Dialogues*, cited in Hans Urs von Balthasar, *The Glory of the Lord:, A Theological Aesthetics,* vol. 5: *The Realm of Metaphysics in the Modern Age* (San Francisco: Ignatius Press, 1991), 95–96.

15. I say "Calvinist" because that is how Law and his contemporaries would identify this theology. Calvin, himself, it should be remembered, says scarcely anything about predestination that one cannot find in the thought of Augustine or Aquinas.

16. An exception is, of course, the reply to Warburton.

17. William Law, *An Appeal to All That Doubt or Disbelieve the Truths of the Gospel, The Works of William Law,* vol. 6 (Eugene, OR: Wipf and Stock, repr., 2001), 153.

18. Ibid., 65.

19. Ibid., 147.

20. Ibid.

21. Ibid., 146.

22. I have deliberately omitted one element in Law's exposition of the person and work of Christ. He argues that the perfection to which Christ will raise us requires that he not only take on our fallen flesh but also have "veiled" under that flesh "an holy humanity of heavenly flesh and blood." "Our common faith, therefore, obliges us to hold, that our Lord had the perfection of the first Adam's flesh and blood united with, and veiled under that fallen nature, which he took upon him from the blessed virgin Mary" (Law, *An Appeal to All That Doubt*, 148). Other than the difficulty of making much sense of this, Law comes dangerously close to undermining the unity of Christ with us "in the flesh." If he possesses a "perfect" body under our fallen body, in what sense does he truly share our condition? This element is not necessary to Law's overall position, and his concern for the redemptive transformation of the flesh is better answered by acknowledging that that transformation takes place in the resurrection.

23. Law varies the form of the metaphors to bring out a variety of biblical associations. Thus we have "ingrafted Word" as well as "in-spoken" and "seed of salvation," "seed of life," "seed of the Woman," "seed of heaven," "heavenly seed," "seed and power of Goodness," "seed of the Word," "seed of God." In all cases the identification with

Christ is clear: "The *Bruiser* of the Serpent, the *Seed* of the Woman, the *Immanuel*, the holy Jesus (for they all mean the same Thing)" (*SL* 405).

24. James Thompson, "On the Memory of Isaac Newton." He really is talking about Isaac Newton, as here:

> The heavens are all his own; from the wild rule
> Of whirling Vortices, and circling Spheres,
> To their first great simplicity restored.

25. *A Letter to Mr. Law: Occasion'd by Reading His Treatise on Christian Perfection; with a Copy of Verses, Address'd to the Same Author. By a Lover of Mankind* (London: printed for W. Hinchliffe, 1728), 22.

26. Law, *An Appeal to All That Doubt*, 126.

27. Ibid., 360.

28. Ibid., 358.

29. William Blake, "The Divine Image," *Songs of Innocence*. Blake had read Law and speaks highly of him as a prophet against the Deists.

30. Law, *Christian Regeneration*, 36.

31. Ibid.

32. Ibid., 37.

33. Ibid., 36.

34. Law, *Address to the Clergy*, 64. Bear in mind here that "*Ages of fiery Pain, and tormenting Darkness*" refers not to punishment as in traditional eschatology but rather to the self-tormenting consequences of sin.

35. Christopher Walton, *Notes and Materials for an Adequate Biography of the Celebrated Divine and Theosopher, William Law* (London: printed for private circulation, 1854), 601.

Index